COOKBOOK

COOKBOOK

PUBLICATIONS INTERNATIONAL, LTD.

Recipe development by the Kraft Kitchens.

On the front cover: "Philly" Cheesecake *(see page 187)*.

On the back cover, left inset *(from top to bottom)*: Pecan Tassies *(see page 110)*, Chocolate "Philly" Fudge *(see page 110)* and "Philly" Apricot Cookies *(see page 108)*.
On the back cover, bottom: Baked Cream Cheese Appetizer *(see page 39)*.

Library of Congress Catalog Number: 88-60998

ISBN: 0-88176-487-6

This edition published by:
Publications International, Ltd.
7373 North Cicero Avenue
Lincolnwood, Illinois 60646

Printed and bound in United States by Arcata Graphics/Hawkins
h g f e d

CONTENTS

AN AMERICAN
ORIGINAL

Cream cheese was developed over 100 years ago and was first produced commercially by an ambitious, hard-working farmer in upstate New York. It was primarily used as a flavorful spread for bread, toast or crackers. Fresh fruit preserves were added to this delightful new cheese giving it a novel taste-twist and creating an almost endless variety of sandwiches and snacks.

This fresh, delicate, creamy-smooth cheese was not used as a recipe ingredient until the mid 1920's. One of the first recipes developed was the "Kraft Philadelphia Cream Cake," which was later retitled "Supreme Cheesecake." Although versions of this original recipe appear In thls book, it was first published in a 1928 Kraft recipe folder and became an instant favorite.

In the late 1940's and early 50's, America discovered cocktail parties and casual home entertaining. Certainly this new life-style helped give birth to appetizers, finger sandwiches and cream cheese dips. These food innovations were so popular that when "Clam Appetizer Dip" was originally featured on the Kraft Music Hall television show, New York City was sold out of canned clams within 24 hours.

We've come a long way from that first "Kraft Philadelphia Cream Cake." The simple cheesecake has matured and grown and become far more glamorous as we marble it with chocolate, top it with meringues, garnish it with kiwi fruit, flavor it with everything from peanut butter to liqueurs.

Today, we've even found a way to make a lighter style of cream cheese with 25% less fat and 20% fewer calories. It's called *Light* PHILADELPHIA BRAND Neufchâtel Cheese. It's similar in taste and texture to regular cream cheese and can be substituted in your favorite cream cheese recipes.

What began as a novel idea—cooking with cream cheese—has become a universally accepted concept. Today, PHILADELPHIA BRAND Cream Cheese is an indispensable ingredient used by great American cooks, like you.

AN AMERICAN
FAVORITE

PHILADELPHIA BRAND Cream Cheese spread on bread, toast, crackers or bagels has always been one of the most popular uses for this most popular product. Today, with *Soft* PHILADELPHIA BRAND Cream Cheese, it's even easier.

Soft "Philly" Cream Cheese is made with the same wholesome ingredients as traditional cream cheese. The fresh, delicate flavor is the same. Significantly different is the consistency which is what makes Soft "Philly" Cream Cheese completely spreadable, even when taken directly from the refrigerator.

Although it was developed and is most often used as a spreading cheese, Soft "Philly" Cream Cheese is suitable for many recipes. You'll especially like it for recipes that require blending with chilled ingredients such as when you're making dips, spreads, frostings, cold sauces or fillings. In recipes designating regular cream cheese, soft cream cheese should not be substituted because a softer consistency may result.

Soft "Philly" Cream Cheese is always ready. Whether you need to quickly satisfy a hungry youngster home from school—or you need to magically make attractive and tasty appetizers suddenly appear for unexpected guests—Soft "Philly" Cream Cheese is the quick and easy answer.

You'll find a number of recipes within this book created especially for Soft PHILADELPHIA BRAND Cream Cheese. Many can be prepared with a minimum of effort and others are more elegant ideas for parties and special entertaining.

GREAT BEGINNINGS

THREE WAY SPLIT SPREADS

1 8-ounce package *Light* PHILADELPHIA
  BRAND Neufchâtel Cheese, softened
2 cups (8 ounces) shredded 100% Natural
  KRAFT Mild Cheddar Cheese
1/3 cup milk
2 tablespoons finely chopped green pepper
2 tablespoons shredded carrot
1 teaspoon grated onion

*   *   *

2 crisply cooked bacon slices, crumbled
1 1/2 teaspoons KRAFT Prepared Horseradish
  (optional)

*   *   *

1/4 teaspoon dill weed
1/8 teaspoon garlic powder
1/8 teaspoon pepper

Combine neufchâtel cheese, cheddar cheese and milk, mixing at medium speed on electric mixer until well blended. Divide mixture into three 2/3-cup portions. To one portion, add green peppers, carrots and onions; mix well.

To second portion, add bacon and horseradish; mix well.

To third portion, add seasonings; mix well.

Arrange cheese spreads on serving tray; serve with crackers.

2 cups

GARLIC SPREAD

1 8-ounce package PHILADELPHIA BRAND
  Cream Cheese, softened
1/2 cup PARKAY Margarine, softened
2 tablespoons chopped parsley
2 tablespoons chopped onion
1 garlic clove, minced

Combine cream cheese and margarine, mixing until well blended. Add remaining ingredients; mix well. Chill.

Approximately 1 2/3 cups

Easy Appetizer Cut-Outs

Easy Appetizer Cut-Outs

1   15-ounce package PILLSBURY All Ready
     Pie Crusts
1   8-ounce package PHILADELPHIA BRAND
     Cream Cheese, softened
1   tablespoon milk
$^1/_2$ teaspoon onion salt
$^1/_2$ teaspoon worcestershire sauce
     Cucumber slices
     Chopped chives
     Dill weed
     Green onion slices
     Radish slices
     Carrot curls
     Pimento slices
     Parsley
     Cleaned small shrimp

Unfold pie crusts; cut out with 2$^1/_2$-inch cutters. Place cut-outs on ungreased cookie sheet; prick each several times with fork. Bake at 425°, 8 to 10 minutes or until golden brown; cool. Combine cream cheese, milk, onion salt and worcestershire sauce, mixing until well blended. Spread on cut-outs; top with remaining ingredients as desired.

2 dozen

ZUCCHINI CHIVE DIP

1 8-ounce container Soft PHILADELPHIA
BRAND Cream Cheese
3 tablespoons milk
1 small zucchini, shredded
3 tablespoons chopped chives
1/8 teaspoon salt

Combine cream cheese and milk, mixing until well blended. Add remaining ingredients; mix well. Chill. Serve with vegetable dippers or chips.

1 cup

IMPROMPTU APPETIZER

1/4 cup SAUCEWORKS Cocktail Sauce
1 8-ounce package PHILADELPHIA BRAND
Cream Cheese
Frozen cooked tiny shrimp, thawed

Pour cocktail sauce over cream cheese; top with shrimp. Serve with crackers or party rye bread slices.

VARIATIONS
Substitute any of the following for cocktail sauce and shrimp:
■ 1/4 cup KRAFT Horseradish Sauce mixed with 1 teaspoon KRAFT Pure Prepared Mustard and finely chopped ham.
■ 2 1/4-ounce can deviled ham and sweet pickle relish.
■ Crisply cooked crumbled bacon and green onion slices.
■ 1/3 cup KRAFT Pineapple Preserves combined with 1/2 teaspoon KRAFT Prepared Horseradish and 1/2 teaspoon KRAFT Pure Prepared Mustard.
■ 1/4 to 1/3 cup chutney.
■ 1/4 cup picante sauce, taco sauce or salsa.

HINT
Keep the ingredients for this quick and delicious recipe on hand for impromptu parties and unexpected guests.

Top: Appetizer Pâté Cheesecake (see page 16)
Center: Zucchini Chive Dip
◄ *Bottom: Impromptu Appetizer*

APPETIZER PÂTÉ CHEESECAKE

1 cup crushed plain croutons
3 tablespoons PARKAY Margarine, melted
* * *
1 envelope unflavored gelatin
1/2 cup cold water
2 8-ounce packages PHILADELPHIA BRAND
     Cream Cheese, softened
1 8-ounce package braunschweiger sausage
     or liver sausage
1/4 cup KRAFT Real Mayonnaise
3 tablespoons chopped pimento
2 tablespoons grated onion
1 tablespoon KRAFT Pure Prepared Mustard
1/2 teaspoon lemon juice

Combine croutons and margarine; press onto bottom of 9-inch springform pan. Bake at 350°, 10 minutes.

Soften gelatin in water; stir over low heat until dissolved. Combine cream cheese and sausage, mixing at medium speed on electric mixer until well blended. Gradually add gelatin. Stir in remaining ingredients until blended; pour over crust. Chill until firm. Remove rim of pan.

16 servings

QUICK MEXICAN SPREAD

1 8-ounce package *Light* PHILADELPHIA
     BRAND Neufchâtel Cheese, softened
1 4-ounce can chopped green chilies, drained

Combine neufchâtel cheese and chilies, mixing until well blended. Chill. Serve with tortilla chips or spread over warm tortillas or corn bread.

1 cup

Petite "Philly" Pinwheels

PETITE "PHILLY" PINWHEELS

1 8-ounce can PILLSBURY Refrigerated
   Quick Crescent Dinner Rolls
   Soft PHILADELPHIA BRAND Cream
   Cheese
1/2 cup finely chopped ham
2 tablespoons finely chopped stuffed green
   olives

Separate dough into four rectangles; firmly press perforations to seal. Spread with cream cheese; sprinkle with ham and olives, pressing lightly. Roll up, starting at short end; seal edges. Cut each roll into four slices. Place, cut-side down, on ungreased cookie sheet; flatten slightly. Bake at 375°, 15 to 17 minutes or until golden brown.

16 appetizers

VARIATION
■ Substitute dried apricots and green pepper for ham and olives.

Fruited Cheese Spread

1 8-ounce package *Light* PHILADELPHIA
    BRAND Neufchâtel Cheese, softened
2 cups (8 ounces) shredded CASINO Brand
    Natural Muenster or Brick Cheese
1/4 cup milk
1/2 cup finely chopped dried apricots
1/4 cup finely chopped green pepper
1/4 teaspoon ground ginger

Combine neufchâtel cheese, muenster cheese and milk, mixing until well blended. Add apricots, green peppers and ginger; mix well. Chill. Serve with party rye or pumpernickel bread slices.

Approximately 2 1/2 cups

VARIATIONS
■ Substitute 1/4 cup finely chopped red pepper and
1 tablespoon finely chopped onion for apricots. Omit ginger.
■ Substitute 100% Natural KRAFT Mild Cheddar Cheese for
Muenster Cheese. Omit apricots and ginger. Add 8 1/4-ounce
can crushed pineapple, well-drained; mix well. Spoon into
serving bowl; chill.
■ Substitute PHILADELPHIA BRAND Cream Cheese for
Neufchâtel Cheese.

Refreshing Cucumber Dip

1 8-ounce package PHILADELPHIA BRAND
    Cream Cheese, softened
1/2 cup sour cream
1 tablespoon milk
1 teaspoon grated onion
1/4 teaspoon worcestershire sauce
1/3 cup finely chopped cucumber

Combine all ingredients except cucumbers, mixing until well blended. Stir in cucumbers. Chill several hours or overnight. Serve with chips or vegetable dippers.

1 2/3 cups

Fruited Cheese Spread ▶

Herb Appetizer Cheesecake

HERB APPETIZER CHEESECAKE

   1 cup dry bread crumbs
¼ cup PARKAY Margarine, melted

*   *   *

¼ cup olive oil
   2 cups fresh basil leaves
½ teaspoon salt
   1 garlic clove, cut in half
   2 8-ounce packages PHILADELPHIA BRAND
      Cream Cheese, softened
   1 cup ricotta cheese
   3 eggs
½ cup (2 ounces) KRAFT Grated Parmesan
      Cheese
½ cup pine nuts

(continued)

Combine crumbs and margarine; press onto bottom of 9-inch springform pan. Bake at 350°, 10 minutes.

Place oil, basil, salt and garlic in blender container. Cover; process on high speed until smooth. Combine basil mixture, cream cheese and ricotta cheese, mixing at medium speed on electric mixer until well blended. Add eggs, one at a time, mixing well after each addition. Blend in parmesan cheese; pour over crust. Top with pine nuts. Bake at 325°, 1 hour and 15 minutes. Loosen cake from rim of pan; cool before removing rim of pan. Serve warm or at room temperature. Garnish with tomato rose and fresh basil, if desired. Chill any remaining cheesecake.

16 servings

VARIATION
■ Substitute 1 cup chopped parsley and 1 tablespoon dried basil leaves for fresh basil leaves.

APPLE CHEDDAR SPREAD

1/4 cup milk

1 8-ounce package *Light* PHILADELPHIA
    BRAND Neufchâtel Cheese, softened

1 cup (4 ounces) 100% Natural KRAFT
    Shredded Mild Cheddar Cheese

1/4 cup finely chopped apple

1/4 cup finely chopped walnuts

1 tablespoon sugar

1/4 teaspoon cinnamon

Gradually add milk to neufchâtel cheese, mixing until well blended. Add remaining ingredients, mixing at medium speed on electric mixer until well blended. Chill. Serve with crackers.

2 cups

COLORFUL CARROT DIP

1 8-ounce package *Light* PHILADELPHIA
  BRAND Neufchâtel Cheese, softened
1/2 cup finely shredded carrot
1 teaspoon parsley flakes
1/8 teaspoon salt
  Dash of pepper

Combine neufchâtel cheese, carrots and seasonings, mixing until well blended. Chill. Serve with vegetable dippers.

1 cup

VARIATIONS

■ Substitute freeze-dried chopped chives for parsley flakes.
■ Substitute 1/2 teaspoon dried basil leaves, crushed, for parsley flakes.
■ Substitute 1/4 teaspoon dill weed or lemon pepper for parsley flakes.

BRAUNSCHWEIGER SAUSAGE SPREAD

1 8-ounce package PHILADELPHIA BRAND
  Cream Cheese, softened
1/2 cup PARKAY Margarine, softened
6 ounces braunschweiger sausage or liver
  sausage
2 tablespoons chopped onion
1 1/2 teaspoons lemon juice
  Dash of worcestershire sauce

Combine cream cheese, margarine and sausage, mixing until well blended. Add remaining ingredients; mix well. Chill.

Approximately 2 1/2 cups

Colorful Carrot Dip ▶

Curried Chicken Puffs

CURRIED CHICKEN PUFFS

1/2 cup water
1/3 cup PARKAY Margarine
2/3 cup flour
   Dash of salt
2 eggs

*　　*　　*

1 8-ounce package PHILADELPHIA BRAND
   Cream Cheese, softened
1/4 cup milk
1/4 teaspoon salt
   Dash of curry powder
   Dash of pepper
1 1/2 cups chopped cooked chicken
1/3 cup slivered almonds, toasted
2 tablespoons green onion slices

(continued)

Bring water and margarine to boil. Add flour and salt; stir vigorously over low heat until mixture forms ball. Remove from heat; add eggs, one at a time, beating until smooth after each addition. Place level measuring tablespoonfuls of batter on ungreased cookie sheet. Bake at 400°, 25 minutes. Cool.

Combine cream cheese, milk, salt, curry powder and pepper, mixing until well blended. Add chicken, almonds and onions; mix lightly. Cut tops from cream puffs; fill with chicken mixture. Replace tops. Place puffs on cookie sheet. Bake at 375°, 5 minutes or until warm.

Approximately 1¹/₂ dozen

NOTE
Unfilled cream puffs can be prepared several weeks in advance and frozen. Place puffs on a jelly roll pan and wrap securely in plastic wrap.

GARDEN VEGETABLE SPREAD

1 8-ounce container Soft PHILADELPHIA
   BRAND Cream Cheese
¹/₂ cup shredded carrot
¹/₂ cup shredded zucchini
1 tablespoon chopped parsley
¹/₄ teaspoon garlic salt
   Dash of pepper

Combine ingredients; mix well. Chill. Serve with party rye or pumpernickel bread slices or assorted crackers.

1¹/₃ cups

VARIATION
■ Serve with LENDER'S Pre-Sliced Frozen Plain Bagelettes, toasted.

HOT BEEF DIP

1/4 cup chopped onion
1 tablespoon PARKAY Margarine
1 cup milk
1 8-ounce package PHILADELPHIA BRAND
    Cream Cheese, cubed
1 3-ounce package smoked sliced beef,
    chopped
1 4-ounce can mushrooms, drained
1/4 cup (1 ounce) KRAFT Grated Parmesan
    Cheese
2 tablespoons chopped parsley

Saute onions in margarine. Add milk and cream cheese; stir over low heat until cream cheese is melted. Add remaining ingredients; heat thoroughly, stirring occasionally. Serve hot with French bread slices, if desired.

2 1/2 cups

VARIATION
■ Substitute 2 1/2-ounce package smoked sliced turkey for 3-ounce package smoked sliced beef.

SERVING SUGGESTION
For a colorful variety, serve with French, whole-wheat or rye bread cubes.

CREAMY DEVILED EGGS

8 hard-cooked eggs
1 8-ounce container Soft PHILADELPHIA
    BRAND Cream Cheese
2 tablespoons sweet pickle relish
1/2 teaspoon dry mustard
1/4 teaspoon salt
    Dash of pepper

Cut eggs in half. Remove yolks; mash. Blend in cream cheese, relish and seasonings, mixing until well blended. Refill whites.

16 deviled eggs

Top: Hot Beef Dip
◄ *Bottom: Pine Nut Cheese Spread (see page 28)*

PINE NUT CHEESE SPREAD

1 8-ounce package PHILADELPHIA BRAND
   Cream Cheese, softened
2 tablespoons KRAFT Grated Parmesan
   Cheese
$1/4$ cup chopped green pepper
1 tablespoon finely chopped onion
2 teaspoons chopped pimento
   Dash of ground red pepper
$1/3$ cup pine nuts or slivered almonds, toasted

Combine all ingredients except pine nuts, mixing until well blended. Chill. Shape into log. Coat with pine nuts just before serving.

1 cup

VARIATION
■ Substitute *Light* PHILADELPHIA BRAND Neufchâtel Cheese for Cream Cheese. Increase Parmesan cheese to $1/4$ cup (1 ounce). Spoon into serving container. Top with pine nuts just before serving.

HINT
Homemade cheese spreads in colorful containers make great hostess gifts. Include the recipe for an added personal touch.

TANGY SPREAD

1 8-ounce package PHILADELPHIA BRAND
   Cream Cheese, softened
$1/2$ cup PARKAY Margarine, softened
$1/4$ cup KRAFT Grated Parmesan Cheese
2 tablespoons dry white wine
2 tablespoons chopped parsley
$1/8$ teaspoon pepper
   Dash of ground thyme
   Dash of garlic powder

Combine cream cheese and margarine, mixing until well blended. Add remaining ingredients; mix well. Chill.

Approximately $1^{2}/_{3}$ cups

SHRIMP APPETIZER CRESCENTS

1 8-ounce package *Light* PHILADELPHIA
    BRAND Neufchâtel Cheese, softened
1 cup finely chopped cooked shrimp
1/3 cup (1 1/2 ounces) KRAFT Grated Parmesan
    Cheese
1 tablespoon milk
2 8-ounce cans PILLSBURY Refrigerated
    Quick Crescent Dinner Rolls
1 egg, beaten
1 teaspoon water

Combine neufchâtel cheese, shrimp, parmesan cheese and milk, mixing until well blended. Separate crescent dough into eight rectangles; firmly press perforations to seal. Spread each rectangle evenly with 2 rounded measuring tablespoonfuls neufchâtel cheese mixture. Cut each rectangle into six triangles; roll as directed on package. Place on greased cookie sheets; brush with combined egg and water. Bake at 375°, 12 to 15 minutes or until golden brown. Serve warm.

4 dozen

VARIATIONS
■ Substitute 6 1/2-ounce can tuna, drained, flaked, for shrimp.
■ Substitute PHILADELPHIA BRAND Cream Cheese for Neufchâtel Cheese.

CLAM APPETIZER DIP

1 8-ounce can minced clams
1 8-ounce package PHILADELPHIA BRAND
    Cream Cheese, softened
2 teaspoons lemon juice
1 1/2 teaspoons worcestershire sauce
1/4 teaspoon garlic salt
    Dash of pepper

Drain clams, reserving 1/4 cup liquid. Combine clams, reserved liquid and remaining ingredients, mixing until well blended. Chill. Serve with potato chips or vegetable dippers.

1 1/2 cups

Hawaiian Coconut Spread

HAWAIIAN COCONUT SPREAD

1 8-ounce container Soft PHILADELPHIA
   BRAND Cream Cheese
2 tablespoons KRAFT Apricot, Pineapple or
   Peach Preserves
1/3 cup flaked coconut

Combine cream cheese and preserves, mixing until well blended. Add coconut;
mix well. Chill. Serve with nut bread slices.

1 1/3 cups

VARIATIONS
■ Add 1/8 teaspoon anise seed.
■ Substitute 1/4 cup whole berry cranberry sauce for KRAFT
Preserves.

APPETIZER PIZZA

1 7.5-ounce can PILLSBURY Refrigerated
  Buttermilk Biscuits
1 medium onion, cut into rings
1 cup chopped zucchini
1 4-ounce can mushrooms, drained
2 tablespoons PARKAY Margarine
1 8-ounce package PHILADELPHIA BRAND
  Cream Cheese, softened
1/4 cup milk
1 egg, beaten
1/2 teaspoon salt

Separate each biscuit into two layers. Place on bottom and sides of greased 12-inch pizza pan, pressing together to form crust. Saute onions, zucchini and mushrooms in margarine. Combine cream cheese, milk, egg and salt, mixing until well blended. Stir in vegetables; pour over crust. Bake at 400°, 20 to 25 minutes or until crust is golden brown. Serve warm.

14 to 16 servings

SIX POINT SPREAD

1 8-ounce package PHILADELPHIA BRAND
  Cream Cheese, softened
1 cup (4 ounces) shredded KRAFT 100%
  Natural Swiss Cheese
4 crisply cooked bacon slices, crumbled
2 tablespoons green onion slices
1 teaspoon worcestershire sauce
2 tablespoons milk

Combine cream cheese and Swiss cheese, mixing at medium speed on electric mixer until well blended. Add remaining ingredients; mix well. Chill. Serve with assorted crackers.

1²/₃ cups

PARTY CHEESE BALL

2 8-ounce packages PHILADELPHIA BRAND
    Cream Cheese, softened
2 cups (8 ounces) shredded CRACKER
    BARREL Brand Sharp Natural Cheddar
    Cheese
1 tablespoon chopped pimento
1 tablespoon chopped green pepper
1 tablespoon finely chopped onion
2 teaspoons worcestershire sauce
1 teaspoon lemon juice
    Dash of ground red pepper
    Dash of salt
    Chopped pecans

Combine cream cheese and cheddar cheese, mixing at medium speed on electric mixer until well blended. Add all remaining ingredients except pecans; mix well. Chill several hours. Shape into ball; roll in pecans. Serve with crackers.

Approximately 2 cups

VARIATIONS
■ Omit pecans. Roll in finely chopped parsley, dried beef or toasted chopped almonds.
■ Shape into log. Coat top and bottom of log with chopped parsley. Slice; serve with crackers or cucumber slices.
■ Shape into 1-inch balls. Roll in chopped nuts, dried beef, toasted sesame seed or chopped parsley.
■ Shape into pyramid. Coat one side with chopped nuts, second side with chopped parsley and third side with chopped dried beef. Serve with party rye bread.
■ Shape into football; coat with pecans. Top with pimento strips to form lacing.

Top: Dill Dip (see page 34)
Bottom: Party Cheese Ball ▶

Dill dip

1 8-ounce package *Light* PHILADELPHIA
 BRAND Neufchâtel Cheese, softened
1/2 cup KRAFT Light Reduced Calorie
 Mayonnaise
3 tablespoons milk
1/4 cup chopped green onion
1 tablespoon chopped parsley
3/4 teaspoon dill weed
1/4 teaspoon celery salt
1/4 teaspoon onion powder

Combine neufchâtel cheese, mayonnaise and milk, mixing until well blended.
Stir in remaining ingredients. Chill. Serve with vegetable dippers.

1 1/2 cups

Picante spread

1 8-ounce package PHILADELPHIA BRAND
 Cream Cheese, softened
1/2 cup PARKAY Margarine, softened
2 tablespoons chopped onion
1 1/2 teaspoons anchovy paste
1 teaspoon KRAFT Pure Prepared Mustard
1 teaspoon chopped capers, drained
1 teaspoon caraway seed
1 teaspoon paprika

Combine cream cheese and margarine, mixing until well blended. Add remaining ingredients; mix well. Chill.

Approximately 1 2/3 cups

Herbed Cheese Pinwheel Canapes

HERBED CHEESE PINWHEEL CANAPES

1 8-ounce package PHILADELPHIA BRAND
   Cream Cheese, softened
2 tablespoons chopped parsley
2 teaspoons lemon juice
1/2 teaspoon dried basil leaves, crushed
1/8 teaspoon pepper
1/8 teaspoon garlic powder
1 1-pound unsliced whole-wheat bread loaf,
   crusts trimmed
   Soft PARKAY Margarine
1/4 cup finely chopped pecans
1/4 cup sesame seed
1 tablespoon worcestershire sauce

Combine cream cheese, parsley, juice and seasonings, mixing until well blended. Slice bread lengthwise into 1/2-inch slices. Roll each slice to 1/4-inch thickness. Evenly spread each bread slice with cream cheese mixture; roll up, starting at narrow end. Spread bread rolls with margarine, excluding ends. In small skillet, combine remaining ingredients; cook 3 minutes or until worcestershire sauce evaporates. Cool. Coat bread rolls with pecan mixture. Cover; chill at least 30 minutes. Cut each bread roll crosswise into 1/2-inch slices.

Approximately 2 1/2 dozen

35

ZESTY HERB SPREAD

1 8-ounce package *Light* PHILADELPHIA
    BRAND Neufchâtel Cheese, softened
1 tablespoon chopped chives
$1/4$ teaspoon dried basil leaves, crushed
    Dash of pepper

Combine ingredients, mixing until well blended. Chill. Using pastry tube, pipe cream cheese mixture onto zucchini slices, red pepper strips, carrot strips and cherry tomatoes.

1 cup

HINT
Keep a crock of Zesty Herb Spread in the refrigerator for unexpected guests or ready-to-eat snacking.

CREAMY GINGER DIP

1 8-ounce package *Light* PHILADELPHIA
    BRAND Neufchâtel Cheese, softened
2 tablespoons orange juice
2 tablespoons KRAFT Orange Marmalade
$1/8$ teaspoon ground ginger
    Assorted fresh fruit

Combine ingredients, mixing until well blended. Chill. Serve with fruit.

1 cup

SERVING SUGGESTION
For a breakfast treat, serve Creamy Ginger Dip with fruit muffins or nut bread.

Top: Zesty Herb Spread
◄ *Bottom: Creamy Ginger Dip*

SAVORY CHEDDAR SPREAD

1 8-ounce package PHILADELPHIA BRAND
    Cream Cheese, softened
1/2 cup MIRACLE WHIP Salad Dressing
1 cup (4 ounces) 100% Natural KRAFT
    Shredded Mild Cheddar Cheese
2 tablespoons green onion slices
8 crisply cooked bacon slices, crumbled
1/2 cup crushed buttery crackers

Combine cream cheese and salad dressing, mixing until well blended. Add cheddar cheese and onions; mix well. Spoon into 9-inch pie plate; sprinkle with combined bacon and crumbs. Bake at 350°, 15 minutes. Serve with additional crackers.

2 cups

VARIATION
■ Substitute 1/4 cup bacon flavored bits for crumbled bacon.

MICROWAVE
Microwave cream cheese on Medium (50%) 30 seconds. Assemble recipe as directed except for sprinkling with bacon and crumbs. Microwave on High 4 minutes or until thoroughly heated, turning dish every 2 minutes. Sprinkle with combined bacon and crumbs. Serve as directed.

APPETIZING TORTILLAS

1 3-ounce package PHILADELPHIA BRAND
    Cream Cheese, softened
2 tablespoons chopped green chilies
    Dash of onion salt
4 flour tortillas
2 tablespoons PARKAY Margarine, melted
    Taco sauce

Combine cream cheese, chilies and onion salt, mixing until well blended. Spread on tortillas; roll up. Place on ungreased cookie sheet; brush with margarine. Bake at 350°, 20 minutes. Serve with taco sauce.

4 appetizers

Baked Cream Cheese Appetizer

BAKED CREAM CHEESE APPETIZER

1 4-ounce package refrigerated crescent
    dinner rolls
1 8-ounce package PHILADELPHIA BRAND
    Cream Cheese
½ teaspoon dill weed
1 egg yolk, beaten

Unroll dough on lightly floured surface; press together seams to form 12×4-inch rectangle. Sprinkle top of cream cheese with half of dill; lightly press dill into cream cheese. Place cream cheese, dill-side down, in center of dough. Sprinkle cream cheese with remaining dill. Enclose cream cheese in dough by bringing sides of dough together, pressing edges to seal. Place on lightly greased cookie sheet; brush with egg yolk. Bake at 350°, 15 to 18 minutes or until lightly browned. Serve with assorted crackers and apple slices.

8 servings

VARIATIONS
■ Substitute combined ½ teaspoon dried rosemary leaves, crushed, and ½ teaspoon paprika for dill weed.
■ Substitute *Light* PHILADELPHIA BRAND Neufchâtel Cheese for Cream Cheese.

CREAMY "PHILLY" GUACAMOLE DIP

2 medium avocados, peeled
1 tablespoon lemon juice
1 8-ounce package PHILADELPHIA BRAND
   Cream Cheese, softened
$1/4$ cup finely chopped onion
$1/2$ teaspoon salt
$1/4$ teaspoon garlic salt
$1/4$ teaspoon hot pepper sauce
1 $10^{1/2}$-ounce can bean dip
Shredded lettuce
Chopped tomato
Ripe olive slices
100% Natural KRAFT Mild Cheddar
   Cheese, shredded

Mash avocados with juice. Combine avocado mixture, cream cheese, onions and seasonings, mixing until well blended. Evenly spread bean dip onto serving platter. Top with remaining ingredients. Serve with avocado mixture and corn or tortilla chips. Garnish with additional chopped tomato and ripe olive slices, if desired.

6 to 8 servings

VARIATION
■ Substitute 16-ounce can refried beans for bean dip.

FILLED NEW POTATOES

2 pounds (18) small new potatoes
1 8-ounce container Soft PHILADELPHIA
   BRAND Cream Cheese
Caviar
Chopped chives

Cook potatoes in boiling salted water 15 to 20 minutes or until tender; drain. Cut thin slice from bottom to form base; scoop out top with melon ball cutter. Fill with cream cheese; top with caviar or chives. Serve warm.

$1^{1/2}$ dozen

Creamy "Philly" Guacamole Dip ▶

Florentine Dip

FLORENTINE DIP

- 1 8-ounce package *Light* PHILADELPHIA BRAND Neufchâtel Cheese, softened
- ½ cup plain yogurt
- 2 tablespoons milk
- 1 10-ounce package frozen spinach, thawed, well-drained, chopped
- 2 hard-cooked eggs, finely chopped
- ¼ teaspoon pepper
- ¼ teaspoon salt

Combine neufchâtel cheese, yogurt and milk, mixing until well blended. Stir in remaining ingredients. Serve with vegetable dippers.

2½ cups

TROPICAL CHEESE BALL

1 8-ounce package PHILADELPHIA BRAND
   Cream Cheese, softened
1 8¼-ounce can crushed pineapple, drained
2 cups (8 ounces) shredded 100% Natural
   KRAFT Mild Cheddar Cheese
½ cup chopped pecans
¼ cup chopped dried apricots
1 teaspoon chopped crystallized ginger
   Flaked coconut

Combine cream cheese and pineapple, mixing until well blended. Add all remaining ingredients except coconut; mix well. Chill several hours. Shape into ball. Roll with coconut.

Approximately 1½ cups

HOT CRABMEAT APPETIZER

1 8-ounce package PHILADELPHIA BRAND
   Cream Cheese, softened
1 7½-ounce can crabmeat, drained, flaked
2 tablespoons finely chopped onion
2 tablespoons milk
½ teaspoon KRAFT Cream Style Horseradish
¼ teaspoon salt
   Dash of pepper
⅓ cup sliced almonds, toasted

Combine all ingredients except almonds, mixing until well blended. Spoon mixture into 9-inch pie plate; sprinkle with almonds. Bake at 375°, 15 minutes. Serve with crackers.

Approximately 1½ cups

VARIATIONS
■ Substitute 8-ounce can minced clams, drained, for crabmeat.
■ Omit almonds; sprinkle with dill weed.

CUCUMBER TEA SANDWICHES

16 white bread slices
1 8-ounce package PHILADELPHIA BRAND
   Cream Cheese, softened
2 tablespoons grated onion
1 medium cucumber, peeled, seeded
2 tablespoons KRAFT Real Mayonnaise
1/8 teaspoon garlic powder

Cut thirty-two bread rounds with 2-inch cutter. Combine cream cheese and onion, mixing until well blended. Shred cucumber; drain thoroughly. Add to combined mayonnaise and garlic powder; mix well. For each sandwich, spread one bread round with rounded measuring tablespoonful of cream cheese mixture. Cover with second bread round; top with teaspoonful of cucumber mixture. Press lightly.

16 sandwiches

CHEESE SPREAD

1 8-ounce package PHILADELPHIA BRAND
   Cream Cheese, softened
1 1/2 cups (6 ounces) 100% Natural KRAFT
   Shredded Sharp Cheddar Cheese
1/2 cup (2 ounces) KRAFT Blue Cheese
   Crumbles
1/2 cup PARKAY Margarine, softened
2 tablespoons milk
2 tablespoons chopped onion
1 teaspoon worcestershire sauce

Combine cheeses and margarine, mixing until well blended. Add remaining ingredients; mix well. Chill.

Approximately 3 cups

Molded Shrimp Spread

1 8-ounce package *Light* PHILADELPHIA
    BRAND Neufchâtel Cheese, softened
1 6-ounce package frozen cooked tiny
    shrimp, thawed, drained
1/4 cup chopped pitted ripe olives
1 2-ounce jar sliced pimento, drained,
    chopped
2 teaspoons lemon juice
1 1/2 teaspoons instant minced onion
1/2 teaspoon worcestershire sauce
1/2 teaspoon hot pepper sauce

Combine ingredients, mixing until well blended. Press mixture into 2-cup bowl. Chill several hours. Unmold. Serve with crackers.

2 cups

VARIATIONS
■ Substitute 6-ounces fresh cleaned shrimp, cooked, finely chopped, for frozen shrimp.
■ Substitute PHILADELPHIA BRAND Cream Cheese for Neufchâtel Cheese.

Sausage in Pastry

1 8-ounce package PHILADELPHIA BRAND
    Cream Cheese, softened
1 cup PARKAY Margarine
2 cups flour
1 pound smoked sausage, cut into 1/2-inch
    pieces

Combine cream cheese and margarine, mixing at medium speed on electric mixer until well blended. Add flour; mix well. Shape into ball; chill. Divide pastry in half. On lightly floured surface, roll each pastry half to 15 × 12-inch rectangle; cut into 3-inch squares. Place sausage piece in center of each pastry square. Bring edges together, pressing to seal. Place on cookie sheet. Bake at 400°, 20 minutes. Serve with SAUCEWORKS Hot Mustard Sauce.

Approximately 40 appetizers

"Philly" Stuffed Mushrooms

"PHILLY" STUFFED MUSHROOMS

2 pounds medium mushrooms
6 tablespoons PARKAY Margarine
1 8-ounce package PHILADELPHIA BRAND
    Cream Cheese, softened
1/2 cup (2 ounces) crumbled KRAFT Natural
    Blue Cheese
2 tablespoons chopped onion

Remove mushroom stems; chop enough stems to measure 1/2 cup. Cook half of mushroom caps in 3 tablespoons margarine over medium heat 5 minutes; drain. Repeat with remaining mushroom caps and margarine. Combine cream cheese and blue cheese, mixing until well blended. Stir in chopped stems and onions; fill mushroom caps. Place on cookie sheet; broil until golden brown.
Approximately 21/2 dozen

SHRIMP SPREAD

1 8-ounce package PHILADELPHIA BRAND
   Cream Cheese, softened

1/2 cup PARKAY Margarine, softened

1/4 cup chili sauce

2 teaspoons prepared horseradish

2 4 1/4-ounce cans small shrimp, drained,
   finely chopped

Combine cream cheese and margarine, mixing until well blended. Add chili sauce and horseradish to cream cheese mixture, mixing until well blended. Add shrimp; mix well. Chill.

Approximately 2 1/2 cups

VARIATION

■ Substitute 1/2 pound cleaned shrimp, cooked, for canned shrimp.

BLUE CHEESE FLAN

3/4 cup crushed buttery crackers

2 tablespoons PARKAY Margarine, melted

*   *   *

2 8-ounce packages PHILADELPHIA BRAND
   Cream Cheese, softened

2 4-ounce packages KRAFT Chopped Blue
   Cheese Crumbles

1 2/3 cups sour cream

3 eggs, beaten

1/8 teaspoon pepper

Combine crumbs and margarine; press onto bottom of 9-inch springform pan. Bake at 350°, 10 minutes.

Combine cream cheese and blue cheese, mixing at medium speed on electric mixer until well blended. Add 2/3 cup sour cream, eggs and pepper; mix well. Pour mixture over crust. Bake at 300°, 45 minutes. Stir remaining sour cream; carefully spread over flan. Continue baking 10 minutes. Loosen flan from rim of pan; cool before removing rim of pan. Chill. Serve with fresh fruit and French bread slices, if desired.

16 servings

MAIN MEAL
MAGIC

CHICKEN TACOS

1 8-ounce package PHILADELPHIA BRAND
  Cream Cheese, cubed
1/3 cup milk
1 1/2 cups chopped cooked chicken
1 4-ounce can chopped green chilies, drained
1/2 teaspoon salt
1/4 teaspoon chili powder or ground cumin
10 taco shells
  Shredded lettuce
  Chopped tomato

Combine cream cheese and milk in saucepan; stir over low heat until smooth. Stir in chicken, chilies and seasonings; heat thoroughly, stirring occasionally. Fill taco shells with meat mixture, lettuce and tomatoes.

10 tacos

TURKEY WITH HERB SAUCE

1 package (approximately 1 1/4 pounds)
  fresh turkey breast slices
1/4 cup flour
1/4 teaspoon salt
2 tablespoons oil

*   *   *

1 8-ounce package *Light* PHILADELPHIA
  BRAND Neufchâtel Cheese, cubed
1/3 cup milk
1 garlic clove, minced
1 teaspoon grated onion
1/4 teaspoon dried oregano leaves, crushed
1/8 teaspoon pepper

Coat turkey with combined flour and salt. Cook turkey on both sides in hot oil over medium-high heat 4 to 6 minutes or until turkey loses pink color.

Combine neufchâtel cheese and milk; stir over low heat until smooth. Stir in garlic, onion and seasonings. Serve over turkey.

4 servings

CREAMY LASAGNE

 1 pound ground beef
 $1/2$ cup chopped onion
 1 $14^1/2$-ounce can tomatoes, cut up
 1 6-ounce can tomato paste
 $1/3$ cup water
 1 garlic clove, minced
 1 teaspoon dried oregano leaves, crushed
 $1/2$ teaspoon salt
 $1/4$ teaspoon pepper
 1 8-ounce package PHILADELPHIA BRAND
    Cream Cheese, cubed
 $1/4$ cup milk
 8 ounces lasagne noodles, cooked, drained
 2 6-ounce packages 100% Natural KRAFT
    Low Moisture Part-Skim Mozzarella
    Cheese Slices
 $1/2$ cup (2 ounces) KRAFT Grated Parmesan
    Cheese

Brown meat in large skillet; drain. Add onions; cook until tender. Stir in tomatoes, tomato paste, water, garlic and seasonings. Cover; simmer 30 minutes. Combine cream cheese and milk in saucepan; stir over low heat until smooth. In 13 x 9-inch baking pan, layer half of noodles, meat mixture, cream cheese mixture, mozzarella and parmesan cheese; repeat layers. Bake at 350°, 30 minutes. Let stand 10 minutes before serving.

6 to 8 servings

MICROWAVE
Crumble meat into 1$1/2$-quart casserole. Microwave on High 4 to 5 minutes or until meat loses pink color when stirred; drain. Add onions, tomatoes, tomato paste, water and seasonings. Cover; microwave 12 minutes, stirring every 3 minutes. Microwave cream cheese and milk in 1-quart measure 3 to 4 minutes or until sauce is hot and smooth, stirring after 1$1/2$ minutes. In 13 x 9-inch baking dish, layer half of noodles, meat mixture, cream cheese mixture, mozzarella and parmesan cheese; repeat with remaining noodles, meat mixture and cream cheese mixture. Microwave 12 minutes, turning dish every 4 minutes. Top with remaining mozzarella and parmesan cheese. Microwave 4 to 6 minutes or until thoroughly heated. Let stand 10 minutes before serving.

TEMPTING CHEESE CREPES

²/₃ cup flour
¹/₂ teaspoon salt
3 eggs, beaten
1 cup milk

* * *

2 8-ounce packages *Light* PHILADELPHIA
   BRAND Neufchâtel Cheese, softened
¹/₄ cup sugar
1 teaspoon vanilla
Strawberry-Banana Topping

Combine flour, salt and eggs; beat until smooth. Gradually add milk, mixing until well blended. For each crepe, pour ¹/₄ cup batter into hot, lightly greased 8-inch skillet or crepe pan, tilting skillet to cover bottom. Cook over medium-high heat until lightly browned on both sides, turning once.

Combine neufchâtel cheese, sugar and vanilla, mixing until well blended. Spread approximately ¹/₄ cup neufchâtel cheese mixture onto each crepe. Fold in thirds. Place in 13×9-inch baking dish. Bake at 350°, 15 to 20 minutes or until thoroughly heated. Serve with Strawberry-Banana Topping.

8 servings

STRAWBERRY-BANANA TOPPING

1 10-ounce package frozen strawberries,
   thawed
1 tablespoon cornstarch
1 banana, sliced

Drain strawberries, reserving liquid. Add enough water to reserved liquid to measure 1¹/₄ cups; gradually add to cornstarch in saucepan, stirring until well blended. Bring to boil over medium heat, stirring constantly. Boil 1 minute. Stir in fruit.

2 cups

PREPARATION TIP
Lightly grease and preheat the skillet or crepe pan until a drop of water sizzles when sprinkled on. If the skillet isn't really hot, crepes may be too thick and stick to the pan.

Top: "Philly" Brunch Quiche,
Spinach Variation (see page 68)
Bottom: Tempting Cheese Crepes ▶

SOUTHWESTERN-STYLE POPOVER

½ pound ground beef
½ cup chopped onion
1 8-ounce package PHILADELPHIA BRAND
   Cream Cheese, cubed
¼ cup water
½ teaspoon salt
½ teaspoon dried oregano leaves, crushed
¼ teaspoon ground cumin

*   *   *

¾ cup flour
½ teaspoon salt
¾ cup milk
2 eggs, beaten
1 tablespoon cornmeal
1 medium tomato, chopped

Brown meat; drain. Add onions; cook until tender. Add cream cheese and water; stir over low heat until cream cheese is melted. Stir in seasonings.

Combine flour, salt, milk and eggs; beat until smooth. Pour into greased 9-inch pie plate; sprinkle with cornmeal. Spoon meat mixture over batter. Bake at 400°, 35 minutes. Top with tomato.

6 to 8 servings

VARIATION
■ Add 4-ounce can chopped green chilies, drained, to meat mixture.

MEXICAN MEATLOAF ROLL

1½ pounds ground beef
¼ cup old fashioned or quick oats, uncooked
2 eggs, beaten
1 tablespoon worcestershire sauce
1 teaspoon pepper
1 8-ounce package PHILADELPHIA BRAND
    Cream Cheese, softened
1 4-ounce can chopped green chilies, drained
¾ cup salsa

Combine meat, oats, eggs, worcestershire sauce and pepper; mix well. On wax paper, press meat mixture into 20 × 10½-inch rectangle. Combine cream cheese and chilies; mix well. Spread cream cheese mixture over meat mixture to within 1-inch of outer edge. Roll, jelly roll fashion, starting at narrow end. Place in 12 × 8-inch baking dish. Bake at 350°, 40 minutes. Top with salsa; continue baking 10 minutes. Let stand 10 minutes before serving.

6 to 8 servings

EGG SALAD MAGNIFIQUE

1 8-ounce package PHILADELPHIA BRAND
    Cream Cheese, softened
½ cup KRAFT Real Mayonnaise
1 tablespoon KRAFT Cream Style Prepared
    Horseradish
6 hard-cooked eggs, chopped
1 6-ounce package frozen crabmeat, thawed,
    drained
½ cup chopped celery
½ cup chopped red or green pepper
6 croissants, split
    Lettuce

Combine cream cheese, mayonnaise and horseradish, mixing until well blended. Add eggs, crabmeat, celery and peppers; mix lightly. Chill. Fill croissants with lettuce and egg mixture.

6 sandwiches

SAUTEED CHICKEN IN CREAM SAUCE

  2 whole chicken breasts, split, boned, skinned
  2 tablespoons PARKAY Margarine
1½ cups mushroom slices
  1 cup celery slices
  1 small onion, thinly sliced
½ teaspoon pepper
½ teaspoon dried basil leaves, crushed
¼ teaspoon dried chervil leaves, crushed
⅛ teaspoon dried thyme leaves, crushed
¼ cup dry white wine or sherry
  1 8-ounce package PHILADELPHIA BRAND Cream Cheese, cubed
⅓ cup milk
2½ cups (8 ounces) tri-colored corkscrew noodles, cooked, drained

Cut chicken into strips. Melt margarine in large skillet; add chicken, vegetables and seasonings. Cook over medium heat, stirring occasionally, 10 minutes or until chicken is tender. Add 2 tablespoons wine; simmer 5 minutes. Combine cream cheese, milk and remaining wine in saucepan; stir over low heat until smooth. To serve, place noodles on serving platter. Top with chicken mixture and cream cheese mixture. Garnish with celery leaves, if desired.

4 to 6 servings

◄ *Sauteed Chicken in Cream Sauce*

CREAMY TURKEY TETRAZZINI

$1/2$ cup chopped onion
$1/2$ cup chopped celery
$1/4$ cup PARKAY Margarine
1 $10^3/4$-ounce can chicken broth
1 8-ounce package PHILADELPHIA BRAND
Cream Cheese, cubed
1 7-ounce package spaghetti, cooked, drained
1 cup chopped cooked turkey
1 4-ounce can mushrooms, drained
2 tablespoons chopped pimento
$1/4$ teaspoon salt
$1/4$ cup (1 ounce) KRAFT Grated Parmesan
Cheese

Saute onions and celery in margarine. Add broth and cream cheese; stir over low heat until cream cheese is melted. Add all remaining ingredients except parmesan cheese; mix lightly. Spoon into $1^1/2$-quart casserole; sprinkle with parmesan cheese. Bake at 350°, 30 minutes.

6 servings

VARIATIONS
■ Substitute chopped cooked chicken for turkey.
■ Dissolve chicken bouillon cube in 1 cup boiling water. Substitute bouillon and water for $10^3/4$-ounce can chicken broth.

SHRIMP A LA PARISIENNE

2 tablespoons PARKAY Margarine, melted
1 pound cleaned shrimp
2 cups mushroom slices
2 tablespoons green onion slices
1 8-ounce package PHILADELPHIA BRAND
Cream Cheese, cubed
$1/4$ cup milk
$1/2$ cup (2 ounces) shredded 100% Natural
KRAFT Swiss Cheese
3 tablespoons dry white wine
2 tablespoons dry bread crumbs

(continued)

Reserve 2 teaspoons melted margarine. Saute shrimp in remaining margarine 3 to 5 minutes or until pink. Add mushrooms and onions; cook until tender. Remove shrimp and mushrooms from pan with slotted spoon; add cream cheese and milk to pan. Stir over low heat until smooth. Add Swiss cheese and wine; stir until cheese is melted. Return shrimp mixture to pan; mix lightly. Spoon into four lightly greased 4-ounce baking dishes. Combine reserved margarine and crumbs. Sprinkle over shrimp mixture. Broil 1 to 2 minutes or until golden brown.

4 servings

VARIATION
■ Substitute 1-quart casserole for four individual baking dishes.

MEXICAN FIESTA PIE

1/2 pound ground beef
1/4 cup chopped onion
  2 teaspoons chili powder
  1 8-ounce package PHILADELPHIA BRAND
     Cream Cheese, cubed
  1 4-ounce can chopped green chilies, drained
1/2 cup pitted ripe olive slices
  2 eggs, beaten

*　　*　　*

3/4 cup flour
1/3 cup milk
  2 eggs, beaten
  1 tablespoon cornmeal
  1 cup chopped tomato
  1 cup (4 ounces) shredded 100% Natural
     KRAFT Mild Cheddar Cheese

Brown meat; drain. Add onions; cook until tender. Stir in chili powder. Add cream cheese, chilies, olives and eggs; mix well.

Combine flour, milk and eggs; beat until smooth. Pour into greased 10-inch pie plate or quiche dish; sprinkle with cornmeal. Spoon meat mixture over batter to within 1/2-inch of outer edge of pan. Bake at 400°, 35 to 40 minutes or until golden brown. Top with tomatoes and cheddar cheese; continue baking 5 minutes.

6 to 8 servings

STROGANOFF SUPERB

1 pound beef sirloin steak, cut into thin
    strips
3 tablespoons PARKAY Margarine
1/2 cup chopped onion
1 4-ounce can mushrooms, drained
1/2 teaspoon salt
1/4 teaspoon dry mustard
1/4 teaspoon pepper
1 8-ounce package PHILADELPHIA BRAND
    Cream Cheese, cubed
3/4 cup milk
    Hot parslied noodles

Brown steak in margarine in large skillet. Add onions, mushrooms and seasonings; cook until vegetables are tender. Add cream cheese and milk; stir over
low heat until cream cheese is melted. Serve over noodles.

4 to 6 servings

SAVORY SUNDAY EGGS

1/4 pound bulk pork sausage
1/2 cup chopped onion
8 eggs, beaten
1/2 cup milk
    Dash of pepper
1 8-ounce package PHILADELPHIA BRAND
    Cream Cheese, cubed
    Chopped chives

Brown sausage in large skillet; drain. Add onions; cook until tender. Add combined eggs, milk and pepper. Cook slowly, stirring occasionally, until eggs be-
gin to set. Add cream cheese; continue cooking, stirring occasionally, until
cream cheese is melted and eggs are set. Sprinkle with chives.

6 servings

Creamy Fettucini Alfredo

CREAMY FETTUCINI ALFREDO

1 8-ounce package PHILADELPHIA BRAND
  Cream Cheese, cubed

³/₄ cup (3 ounces) KRAFT Grated Parmesan
  Cheese

¹/₂ cup PARKAY Margarine

¹/₂ cup milk

8 ounces fettucini, cooked, drained

In large saucepan, combine cream cheese, parmesan cheese, margarine and milk; stir over low heat until smooth. Add fettucini; toss lightly.

4 servings

CREAMY TUNA ON BAGELS

    1 8-ounce package PHILADELPHIA BRAND
        Cream Cheese, softened
    1 6$^{1}/_{2}$-ounce can tuna, drained, flaked
    2 tablespoons green onion slices
$^{1}/_{2}$ teaspoon dill weed
        Dash of pepper
    3 LENDER'S Pre-Sliced Frozen Bagels,
        toasted

Combine all ingredients except bagels; mix lightly. Spread bagel halves with cream cheese mixture. Broil 5 to 7 minutes or until thoroughly heated.

6 servings

VARIATION
■ Substitute 6$^{3}/_{4}$-ounce can chunk ham, drained, flaked, for tuna.

LAYERED CHICKEN SALAD

    1 8-ounce package *Light* PHILADELPHIA
        BRAND Neufchâtel Cheese, softened
    2 medium avocados, peeled, mashed
$^{1}/_{4}$ cup milk
    1 tablespoon lemon juice
    1 tablespoon chopped onion
$^{1}/_{2}$ teaspoon salt
    4 cups shredded lettuce
    1 cup chopped red or green pepper
    2 cups chopped cooked chicken
    1 11-ounce can mandarin orange segments,
        drained
    4 crisply cooked bacon slices, crumbled

Combine neufchâtel cheese, avocados, milk and juice, mixing until well blended. Add onions and salt; mix well. In 2$^{1}/_{2}$-quart glass serving bowl, layer lettuce, peppers, chicken and oranges. Spread neufchâtel cheese mixture over oranges to cover. Chill. Top with bacon just before serving.

6 to 8 servings

"PHILLY" KABOBS

2/3 cup KRAFT "Zesty" Italian Dressing

1 1/2 pounds round steak, cut into strips

1/4 cup chopped onion

1 tablespoon PARKAY Margarine

1 8-ounce package PHILADELPHIA BRAND
Cream Cheese, cubed

3/4 cup milk

1/4 cup (1 ounce) KRAFT Grated Parmesan
Cheese

1/4 teaspoon dry mustard

2 cups summer squash, cut into 1/2-inch
slices

1 cup cherry tomatoes

Hot cooked rice

Pour dressing over steak. Cover; marinate in refrigerator several hours or over-night. Drain, reserving dressing. Saute onions in margarine. Add cream cheese and milk; stir over low heat until cream cheese is melted. Stir in parmesan cheese and mustard.

Indoors

Thread steak and vegetables accordian style on skewers; place on rack of broiler pan. Broil 8 to 10 minutes or to desired doneness, brushing frequently with reserved dressing and turning occasionally. Serve over rice. Top with cream cheese mixture.

Outdoors

Thread steak and vegetables accordian style on skewers; place on greased grill over hot coals (coals will be glowing). Grill, uncovered, to desired doneness, brushing frequently with reserved dressing and turning occasionally. Serve over rice. Top with cream cheese mixture.

6 servings

FESTIVE CHICKEN SALAD

1 8 1/4-ounce can crushed pineapple,
  undrained
1 8-ounce container Soft PHILADELPHIA
  BRAND Cream Cheese
2 cups chopped cooked chicken
1 8-ounce can water chestnuts, drained,
  sliced
1/2 cup celery slices
1/2 cup slivered almonds, toasted
1/4 cup green onion slices
1/4 teaspoon salt
  Dash of pepper
4 medium tomatoes
  Lettuce

Drain pineapple, reserving 1/4 cup liquid. Combine reserved liquid and cream cheese, mixing until well blended. Add pineapple, chicken, water chestnuts, celery, 1/4 cup almonds, onions, salt and pepper; mix lightly. Chill. Cut each tomato into six wedges, almost to stem end. Fill with chicken mixture. Sprinkle with remaining almonds. Serve on lettuce-lined plates.

4 servings

VARIATIONS
■ Omit tomatoes; serve salad over honeydew or cantaloupe wedges or in lettuce cups.
■ Substitute chopped pecans for almonds.

Festive Chicken Salad ▶

HAM AND CHEESE STRATA

12 white bread slices

1½ cups (6 ounces) shredded 100% Natural KRAFT Mild Cheddar Cheese

1 10-ounce package frozen chopped broccoli, thawed, well-drained

1 cup chopped ham

1 8-ounce package PHILADELPHIA BRAND Cream Cheese, softened

3 eggs

1 cup milk

½ teaspoon dry mustard

Place six bread slices on bottom of 12 × 8-inch baking dish. Cover with 1 cup cheddar cheese, broccoli, ham and remaining bread slices, cut in half diagonally. Beat cream cheese until light and fluffy. Add eggs, one at a time, mixing well after each addition. Blend in milk and mustard; pour over bread. Top with remaining cheddar cheese. Bake at 350°, 45 to 50 minutes or until set. Let stand 10 minutes before serving.

6 servings

SMOKED BEEF DIJON

1 8-ounce package PHILADELPHIA BRAND Cream Cheese, cubed

½ cup milk

1 tablespoon dijon mustard

1 tablespoon KRAFT Prepared Horseradish

1 4-ounce package smoked sliced beef, chopped

1 7-ounce package frozen puff pastry shells, baked

In saucepan, combine cream cheese, milk, mustard and horseradish; stir over low heat until smooth. Stir in beef. Serve in pastry shells.

6 servings

◄ *Ham and Cheese Strata*

"PHILLY" BRUNCH QUICHE

Pastry for 1-crust 10-inch pie

* * *

1 8-ounce package PHILADELPHIA BRAND
   Cream Cheese, cubed
1 cup milk
4 eggs, beaten
1/4 cup chopped onion
1 tablespoon PARKAY Margarine
1 cup finely chopped ham
1/4 cup chopped pimento
1/4 teaspoon dill weed
   Dash of pepper

On lightly floured surface, roll pastry to 12-inch circle. Place in 10-inch pie plate. Turn under edge; flute. Prick bottom and sides of pastry with fork. Bake at 400°, 12 to 15 minutes or until pastry is lightly browned.

Combine cream cheese and milk in saucepan; stir over low heat until smooth. Gradually add cream cheese mixture to eggs, mixing until well blended. Saute onions in margarine. Add onions and remaining ingredients to cream cheese mixture; mix well. Pour into pastry shell. Bake at 350°, 35 to 40 minutes or until set. Garnish with ham slices and fresh dill, if desired.

8 servings

VARIATIONS
■ Substitute 1/4 cup finely chopped green pepper for dill weed.
■ Substitute 10-ounce package frozen chopped spinach, cooked, drained, 1 cup (4 ounces) shredded KRAFT 100% Natural Swiss Cheese and 6 crisply cooked bacon slices, crumbled, for ham, pimento and dill weed.
■ Substitute 4-ounce package pepperoni slices, chopped, 1/4 cup (1 ounce) KRAFT Grated Parmesan Cheese and 1/2 teaspoon dried oregano leaves, crushed, for ham, pimento and dill weed. Place pepperoni on bottom of baked pastry shell; continue as directed.

"Philly" Brunch Quiche ▶

STRAWBERRY FRENCH TOAST

1 10-ounce package frozen strawberries,
   thawed
$1/2$ cup sugar
2 tablespoons cornstarch
$1/2$ cup sliced almonds, toasted

*   *   *

1 8-ounce package PHILADELPHIA BRAND
   Cream Cheese, softened
2 tablespoons sugar
1 teaspoon vanilla
1 15×5-inch Italian bread loaf
6 eggs, beaten
$1/3$ cup milk
$1/4$ teaspoon ground nutmeg
   PARKAY Margarine

Drain strawberries, reserving liquid. Add water to reserved liquid to measure 1 cup. Combine sugar and cornstarch in saucepan; gradually add liquid. Cook, stirring constantly, until mixture is clear and thickened. Stir in strawberries and almonds.

Combine cream cheese, sugar and vanilla, mixing until well blended. Cut bread into $1^1/2$-inch slices. Cut slit through crust of each slice to form pocket. Fill each pocket with 1 rounded measuring tablespoonful of cream cheese mixture. Dip each bread slice into combined eggs, milk and nutmeg. Grill both sides in margarine until golden brown. Serve with strawberry mixture.

10 servings

VARIATION
■ Substitute $8^1/4$-ounce can crushed pineapple for strawberries.

FLANK STEAK BEARNAISE

1 8-ounce package PHILADELPHIA BRAND
   Cream Cheese, cubed
¼ cup milk
1 tablespoon green onion slices
½ teaspoon dried tarragon leaves, crushed
2 egg yolks, beaten
2 tablespoons dry white wine
1 tablespoon lemon juice
1 1½-pound beef flank steak

In saucepan, combine cream cheese, milk, green onions and tarragon; stir over low heat until cream cheese is melted. Stir small amount of hot cream cheese mixture into egg yolks; return to hot mixture. Stir in wine and juice. Cook, stirring constantly, over low heat 1 minute or until thickened. Score steak on both sides. Place on rack of broiler pan. Broil on both sides to desired doneness. With knife slanted, carve steak across grain into thin slices. Serve with cream cheese mixture.

6 servings

CREAMY PASTA PRIMAVERA

½ cup chopped green onion
½ cup red and green pepper strips
1 4-ounce can mushrooms, drained
⅓ cup PARKAY Margarine
1 8-ounce package PHILADELPHIA BRAND
   Cream Cheese, cubed
¾ cup milk
2 cups ham cubes
⅓ cup (1½ ounces) KRAFT Grated Parmesan
   Cheese
1 7-ounce package spaghetti, cooked, drained

Saute vegetables in ¼ cup margarine. Add cream cheese and milk; stir over low heat until cream cheese is melted. Stir in ham and parmesan cheese. Toss spaghetti with remaining margarine. Add cream cheese mixture; mix lightly. Serve immediately.

6 servings

SUPERB SIDE DISHES

SAVORY SPINACH CASSEROLE

    1 8-ounce package *Light* PHILADELPHIA
       BRAND Neufchâtel Cheese, softened
 1/4 cup milk
    2 10-ounce packages frozen chopped
       spinach, cooked, drained
 1/3 cup (1 1/2 ounces) KRAFT Grated Parmesan
       Cheese

Combine neufchâtel cheese and milk, mixing until well blended. Spoon spinach into 1-quart casserole; top with neufchâtel cheese mixture. Sprinkle with parmesan cheese. Bake at 350°, 20 minutes.

4 to 6 servings

VARIATION
■ Substitute PHILADELPHIA BRAND Cream Cheese for Neufchâtel Cheese.

MICROWAVE
Prepare casserole as directed except for baking. Microwave on High 4 1/2 to 5 minutes or until hot.

FRESH AND CREAMY POTATO SALAD

    4 cups cubed cooked potato
 1/2 cup celery slices
 1/4 cup chopped green pepper
    2 tablespoons green onion slices
    1 teaspoon salt
    1 8-ounce package PHILADELPHIA BRAND
       Cream Cheese, softened
 1/2 cup sour cream
    2 tablespoons milk

Combine potatoes, celery, green peppers, onions and salt; mix lightly. Combine cream cheese, sour cream and milk, mixing until well blended. Add to potato mixture; mix lightly. Chill.

6 to 8 servings

Creamy Topped Fruit Salad

CREAMY TOPPED FRUIT SALAD

1 8-ounce package *Light* PHILADELPHIA
    BRAND Neufchâtel Cheese, softened
2 tablespoons lemon juice
1 teaspoon grated lemon peel
1/2 cup whipping cream
1/4 cup powdered sugar
2 cups peach slices
2 cups blueberries
2 cups strawberry slices
2 cups grapes

Combine neufchâtel cheese, juice and peel, mixing until well blended. Beat whipping cream until soft peaks form; gradually add sugar, beating until stiff peaks form. Fold into neufchâtel cheese mixture; chill. Layer fruit in 2½-quart glass serving bowl. Top with neufchâtel cheese mixture. Sprinkle with nuts, if desired. Chill.

8 servings

VARIATION
■ Substitute PHILADELPHIA BRAND Cream Cheese for Neufchâtel Cheese.

GARDEN MACARONI SALAD

1/4 cup KRAFT Real Mayonnaise
1 8-ounce package PHILADELPHIA BRAND
    Cream Cheese, softened
1/4 cup sweet pickle relish, drained
1 tablespoon KRAFT Pure Prepared Mustard
2 cups (7 ounces) elbow macaroni, cooked,
    drained
1 cup chopped cucumber
1/2 cup chopped green pepper
1/2 cup radish slices
2 tablespoons chopped onion
1/2 teaspoon salt

Gradually add mayonnaise to cream cheese, mixing until well blended. Stir in relish and mustard. Add remaining ingredients; mix lightly. Spoon into lightly oiled 9-inch springform pan with ring insert. Chill several hours or overnight. Unmold. Garnish with cucumber slices and radish roses, if desired.

6 to 8 servings

VARIATION
■ Add 1/2 cup (2 ounces) KRAFT Grated Parmesan Cheese to cream cheese mixture.

"PHILLY" CHIVE SAUCE

1 8-ounce package *Light* PHILADELPHIA
    BRAND Neufchâtel Cheese, cubed
1/2 cup milk
1 tablespoon chopped chives
1 teaspoon lemon juice
1/4 teaspoon garlic salt

Combine neufchâtel cheese and milk in saucepan; stir over low heat until smooth. Stir in remaining ingredients. Serve over hot cooked potatoes, green beans, broccoli or asparagus.

1 1/3 cups

Garden Macaroni Salad ▶

SPARKLING CHERRY MOLD

    1 17-ounce can pitted dark sweet cherries,
        undrained
    1 3-ounce package cherry flavored gelatin
    1 cup boiling water
    1 cup ginger ale

*   *   *

    1 3-ounce package cherry flavored gelatin
    1 cup boiling water
    1 8-ounce package PHILADELPHIA BRAND
        Cream Cheese, softened
        Lettuce

Drain cherries, reserving 3/4 cup liquid. Dissolve gelatin in water; add ginger ale. Chill until thickened but not set; fold in cherries. Pour into lightly oiled 1 1/2-quart mold; chill until almost set.

Dissolve gelatin in water; add reserved liquid. Gradually add gelatin mixture to cream cheese, mixing at medium speed on electric mixer until well blended. Pour over molded layer; chill until firm. Unmold onto lettuce-lined serving plate.

6 to 8 servings

CREAMY NECTARINE MOLD WITH STRAWBERRY SAUCE

    1 envelope unflavored gelatin
  1/2 cup cold water
    1 8-ounce package PHILADELPHIA BRAND
        Cream Cheese, softened
  1/2 cup sugar
  1/2 cup milk
    2 tablespoons orange flavored liqueur
    1 cup whipping cream, whipped
    1 nectarine, sliced

*   *   *

    1 pint strawberries, sliced
  1/4 cup sugar
    1 tablespoon orange flavored liqueur

(continued)

Soften gelatin in water; stir over low heat until dissolved. Combine cream cheese and sugar, mixing until well blended. Gradually add gelatin, milk and liqueur, mixing until blended. Fold in whipped cream. Spoon ¼ cup cream cheese mixture into lightly oiled 1-quart mold. Arrange nectarines on cream cheese mixture; top with remaining cream cheese mixture. Chill until firm. Unmold onto serving plate.

Combine strawberries, sugar and liqueur; let stand 10 minutes. Serve with mold.

6 to 8 servings

VARIATION
■ Substitute orange juice for orange flavored liqueur. Add 1 teaspoon grated orange peel to cream cheese mixture.

CREAM CHEESE KUGEL

1 8-ounce package PHILADELPHIA BRAND Cream Cheese, softened
¼ cup PARKAY Margarine, melted
4 eggs, beaten
½ cup milk
¼ cup sugar
½ teaspoon salt
4 cups (8 ounces) fine noodles, cooked, drained
½ cup raisins
¼ teaspoon cinnamon

Combine cream cheese and margarine, mixing until well blended. Blend in eggs, milk, sugar and salt. Add noodles and raisins; mix well. Pour mixture into 12 × 8-inch baking dish. Sprinkle with cinnamon. Bake at 375°, 30 minutes or until set.

6 to 8 servings

VARIATION
■ Substitute 8¼-ounce can crushed pineapple, drained, for raisins.

MICROWAVE
Prepare recipe as directed except for baking. Microwave on High 8 minutes, turning dish after 4 minutes. Microwave on Medium (50%) 9 to 12 minutes or until center is set.

Fruit Salad Supreme

1 8-ounce package PHILADELPHIA BRAND
   Cream Cheese, softened
$1/4$ cup milk
1 tablespoon lemon juice
$1/2$ teaspoon grated lemon peel
1 cup whipping cream
$1/2$ cup powdered sugar
4 cups apple slices
3 cups honeydew chunks
3 cups green grapes
$1/2$ cup chopped pecans

Combine cream cheese, milk, juice and peel, mixing until well blended. Beat whipping cream until soft peaks form; gradually add sugar, beating until stiff peaks form. Fold whipped cream mixture into cream cheese mixture. Combine $1/2$ cup cream cheese mixture and apples; mix lightly. In 3-quart glass bowl, layer honeydew, apple mixture and grapes. Top with remaining cream cheese mixture; sprinkle with pecans.

12 servings

Homespun Scalloped Potatoes

1 8-ounce package PHILADELPHIA BRAND
   Cream Cheese, cubed
$1^{1}/4$ cups milk
$1/2$ teaspoon salt
$1/8$ teaspoon pepper
4 cups thin potato slices
2 tablespoons chopped chives

In large saucepan, combine cream cheese, milk, salt and pepper; stir over low heat until smooth. Add potatoes and chives; mix lightly. Spoon into $1^{1}/2$-quart casserole; cover. Bake at 350°, 1 hour and 10 minutes or until potatoes are tender. Stir before serving.

6 servings

MAKE AHEAD
Prepare as directed except for baking. Cover; refrigerate overnight. When ready to serve, bake as directed.

Vegetable Stir-Fry

VEGETABLE STIR-FRY

1 8-ounce package *Light* PHILADELPHIA
   BRAND Neufchâtel Cheese, cubed

1/4 cup sesame seed, toasted

2 cups diagonally-cut carrot slices

2 cups diagonally-cut celery slices

3/4 cup thin green pepper strips

2 tablespoons PARKAY Margarine

1/4 teaspoon salt

   Dash of pepper

Coat neufchâtel cheese cubes with sesame seed; chill. In large skillet or wok, stir-fry vegetables in margarine and seasonings until crisp-tender. Remove from heat. Add neufchâtel cheese to vegetables; mix lightly.

6 to 8 servings

VARIATION

■ Substitute PHILADELPHIA BRAND Cream Cheese for Neufchâtel Cheese.

SHRIMP CHOWDER

    ½ cup celery slices
    ⅓ cup finely chopped onion
    2 tablespoons PARKAY Margarine
    1 8-ounce package PHILADELPHIA BRAND
       Cream Cheese, cubed
    1 cup milk
 1 ½ cups cubed cooked potato
    1 6-ounce package frozen cooked tiny
       shrimp, thawed, drained
    2 tablespoons dry white wine
    ½ teaspoon salt

Saute celery and onions in margarine. Add cream cheese and milk; stir over low heat until cream cheese is melted. Add remaining ingredients; heat thoroughly, stirring occasionally.

Approximately four 1-cup servings

CREAMY RICE PILAF

    2 beef bouillon cubes
 2¼ cups boiling water
    1 cup regular long grain rice
    1 cup carrot slices
    2 tablespoons green onion slices
    1 tablespoon PARKAY Margarine
    ½ teaspoon dill weed
    1 8-ounce package PHILADELPHIA BRAND
       Cream Cheese, cubed
    2 tablespoons KRAFT Real Mayonnaise

Dissolve bouillon in water in saucepan; add rice, vegetables, margarine and dill weed. Cover; simmer 20 minutes or until water is absorbed and rice is tender. Remove from heat. Add cream cheese and mayonnaise; stir until cream cheese is melted.

6 servings

Shrimp Chowder ▶

Stuffed Squash

STUFFED SQUASH

1/4 cup slivered almonds

1 tablespoon PARKAY Margarine

1 8-ounce package *Light* PHILADELPHIA BRAND Neufchâtel Cheese, cubed

3/4 cup milk

1 10-ounce package frozen cut green beans, cooked, drained

1/2 cup water chestnuts, sliced

1 1/2 teaspoons lemon juice

1/2 teaspoon dry mustard

1/4 teaspoon ground ginger

1/4 teaspoon salt

2 acorn squash, cut in half, baked

(continued)

Saute almonds in margarine in saucepan until lightly browned. Add neufchâtel cheese and milk; stir over low heat until neufchâtel cheese is melted. Stir in all remaining ingredients except squash; heat thoroughly, stirring occasionally. Spoon vegetable mixture into hot squash.

4 servings

NOTES
To bake acorn squash: Cut squash lengthwise into halves; scoop out seeds. Place squash, cut-side down, in 13 × 9-inch baking pan. Add enough hot water to measure ½-inch up sides of pan. Bake at 375°, 45 to 55 minutes, or until squash is tender.

Omit squash. Prepare vegetable mixture as directed. Spoon vegetable mixture over 4 cups hot cooked noodles.

LAYERED SALAD EXTRAORDINAIRE

  1 8-ounce package *Light* PHILADELPHIA
      BRAND Neufchâtel Cheese, softened
¾ cup (3 ounces) crumbled KRAFT Natural
      Blue Cheese
¼ cup KRAFT Light Reduced Calorie
      Mayonnaise
¼ cup milk
  2 tablespoons lemon juice
  1 tablespoon chopped chives

            *   *   *

  2 quarts torn assorted greens
  1 cup shredded carrot
2½ cups ham cubes
  1 cup chopped green pepper
  2 cups chopped tomato

Combine neufchâtel cheese and blue cheese, mixing until well blended. Add mayonnaise, milk, juice and chives; mix well.

Combine greens and carrots. Combine meat and green peppers. In 3-quart bowl, layer greens mixture, tomatoes and meat mixture. Spread neufchâtel cheese mixture over meat mixture to seal. Cover; chill several hours.

8 servings

BOUNTIFUL BREADS

FAVORITE BANANA BREAD

1 8-ounce package PHILADELPHIA BRAND
   Cream Cheese, softened
1 cup sugar
1/4 cup PARKAY Margarine
1 cup mashed ripe banana
2 eggs
2 1/4 cups flour
1 1/2 teaspoons baking powder
1/2 teaspoon baking soda
1 cup chopped nuts

Combine cream cheese, sugar and margarine, mixing until well blended. Blend in banana and eggs. Add combined remaining ingredients, mixing just until moistened. Pour into greased and floured 9 × 5-inch loaf pan. Bake at 350°, 1 hour and 10 minutes or until wooden pick inserted near center comes out clean. Cool 5 minutes; remove from pan. Serve with additional cream cheese, if desired.

1 loaf

EASY CHEESE DANISH

1 5-ounce can refrigerated buttermilk flaky
   biscuits
Soft PHILADELPHIA BRAND Cream
   Cheese with Strawberries or Pineapple
Flaked coconut

Separate dough into five biscuits. Make wide indentation in center of each biscuit; fill with measuring tablespoonful of cream cheese. Sprinkle with coconut. Bake at 375°, 12 to 15 minutes or until golden brown. Serve warm.

5 servings

VARIATION
■ Substitute Soft PHILADELPHIA BRAND Cream Cheese for Cream Cheese with Strawberries. Omit coconut. Sprinkle with cinnamon-sugar after baking.

Prune walnut coffeecake

3/4 cup water
1 tablespoon lemon juice
1 1/2 cups chopped pitted prunes

* * *

1 8-ounce package PHILADELPHIA BRAND
Cream Cheese, softened
1 cup granulated sugar
1/2 cup PARKAY Margarine
2 eggs
1 teaspoon vanilla
1 3/4 cups flour
1 teaspoon baking powder
1/2 teaspoon baking soda
1/4 teaspoon salt
1/4 cup milk
1/2 cup chopped walnuts

* * *

1 cup sifted powdered sugar
1 to 2 tablespoons milk

Place water, juice and prunes in blender container. Cover; process until well blended.

Combine cream cheese, granulated sugar and margarine, mixing until well blended. Blend in eggs and vanilla. Add combined dry ingredients alternately with milk, mixing well after each addition. Spread 2 cups batter into greased and floured 13 × 9-inch baking pan. Cover batter with prune mixture; carefully spread with remaining batter. Sprinkle with walnuts. Bake at 350°, 50 minutes. Cool.

Combine powdered sugar and milk; mix well. Drizzle over cake.

12 servings

PUMPKIN CHEESE BREAD

2½ cups sugar
1 8-ounce package PHILADELPHIA BRAND
    Cream Cheese, softened
½ cup PARKAY Margarine
4 eggs
1 16-ounce can pumpkin
3½ cups flour
2 teaspoons baking soda
1 teaspoon salt
1 teaspoon cinnamon
½ teaspoon baking powder
¼ teaspoon ground cloves
1 cup chopped nuts

Combine sugar, cream cheese and margarine, mixing at medium speed on electric mixer until well blended. Add eggs, one at a time, mixing well after each addition. Blend in pumpkin. Add combined dry ingredients, mixing just until moistened. Fold in nuts. Pour into two greased and floured 9 × 5-inch loaf pans. Bake at 350°, 1 hour or until wooden pick inserted in center comes out clean. Cool 5 minutes; remove from pans.   *2 loaves*

CRULLERS

1 8-ounce package PHILADELPHIA BRAND
    Cream Cheese, softened
⅓ cup PARKAY Margarine
1 cup flour
Dash of salt
Sugar

Combine cream cheese and margarine, mixing until well blended. Add flour and salt; mix well. Shape dough into ball; chill 1 hour. On lightly floured surface, roll dough to 12 × 6-inch rectangle. Cut dough into twenty-four ½-inch strips. Fry in deep hot oil, 375°, 1 to 2 minutes or until golden brown, turning once using tongs. Drain on paper towels. Roll in sugar.

2 dozen

Pumpkin Cheese Bread ▶

Apricot Crumble Cake

APRICOT CRUMBLE CAKE

   1 8-ounce package PHILADELPHIA BRAND
      Cream Cheese, softened
  $1/2$ cup PARKAY Margarine
$1^1/4$ cups granulated sugar
  $1/4$ cup milk
   2 eggs
   1 teaspoon vanilla
$1^3/4$ cups flour
   1 teaspoon baking powder
  $1/2$ teaspoon baking soda
  $1/4$ teaspoon salt
   1 10-ounce jar KRAFT Apricot or Peach
      Preserves

        *   *   *

   2 cups flaked coconut
 $2/3$ cup packed brown sugar
   1 teaspoon cinnamon
 $1/3$ cup PARKAY Margarine, melted

(continued)

Combine cream cheese, margarine and granulated sugar, mixing at medium speed on electric mixer until well blended. Gradually add milk, mixing well after each addition. Blend in eggs and vanilla. Add combined dry ingredients to cream cheese mixture; mix well. Pour half of batter into greased and floured 13 × 9-inch baking pan. Dot with preserves; cover with remaining batter. Bake at 350°, 35 to 40 minutes or until wooden pick inserted in center comes out clean.

Combine coconut, brown sugar, cinnamon and margarine; mix well. Spread onto cake; broil 3 to 5 minutes, or until golden brown.

16 servings

FRUITY SWIRL COFFEECAKE

        1 8-ounce package PHILADELPHIA BRAND
            Cream Cheese, softened
        1 cup sugar
      1/2 cup PARKAY Margarine
        2 eggs
      1/2 teaspoon vanilla
    1 3/4 cups flour
        1 teaspoon baking powder
      1/2 teaspoon baking soda
      1/4 teaspoon salt
      1/4 cup milk
      1/2 cup KRAFT Red Raspberry Preserves

Combine cream cheese, sugar and margarine, mixing until well blended. Add eggs, one at a time, mixing well after each addition. Blend in vanilla. Add combined dry ingredients alternately with milk, mixing well after each addition. Pour into greased and floured 13 × 9-inch baking pan; dot with preserves. Cut through batter with knife several times for marble effect. Bake at 350°, 35 minutes.

12 servings

TREASURE BRAN MUFFINS

1¼ cups whole bran cereal
1 cup milk
¼ cup oil
1 egg, beaten
1¼ cups flour
½ cup sugar
1 tablespoon baking powder
½ teaspoon salt
½ cup raisins

* * *

1 8-ounce package PHILADELPHIA BRAND
Cream Cheese, softened
¼ cup sugar
1 egg, beaten

Combine cereal and milk; let stand 2 minutes. Add combined oil and egg; mix well. Add combined dry ingredients, mixing just until moistened. Stir in raisins. Spoon into greased and floured medium-size muffin pan, filling each cup ²/₃ full.

Combine cream cheese, sugar and egg, mixing until well blended. Drop rounded measuring tablespoonfuls of cream cheese mixture onto batter. Bake at 375°, 25 minutes. *1 dozen*

RAISIN SCONES

1 8-ounce package PHILADELPHIA BRAND
Cream Cheese, softened
½ cup sugar
⅓ cup raisins
1 teaspoon grated lemon peel

* * *

3 cups flour
1 tablespoon baking powder
1½ teaspoons salt
½ cup PARKAY Margarine
1 cup milk
Honey

(continued)

Combine cream cheese and sugar, mixing until well blended. Add raisins and peel; mix well.

Combine dry ingredients; cut in margarine until mixture resembles coarse crumbs. Add milk, mixing just until moistened. Divide dough in half. On lightly floured surface, roll out each half to 12 × 9-inch rectangle. Spread one rectangle with cream cheese mixture; top with remaining dough. Cut into twelve 3-inch squares; cut each square in half diagonally. Place on ungreased cookie sheet. Bake at 425°, 12 to 15 minutes or until lightly browned. Drizzle with honey.

2 dozen

CINNAMON STREUSEL COFFEECAKE

$1/2$ cup chopped nuts
$1/3$ cup packed brown sugar
$1/4$ cup flour
$1/2$ teaspoon cinnamon
$1/4$ cup PARKAY Margarine

* * *

1 8-ounce package PHILADELPHIA BRAND Cream Cheese, softened
1 cup granulated sugar
$1/2$ cup PARKAY Margarine
2 eggs
1 teaspoon vanilla
$1^3/4$ cups flour
1 teaspoon baking powder
$1/2$ teaspoon baking soda
$1/4$ teaspoon salt
$1/4$ cup milk

Combine nuts, brown sugar, flour and cinnamon; cut in margarine until mixture resembles coarse crumbs.

Combine cream cheese, granulated sugar and margarine, mixing at medium speed on electric mixer until well blended. Blend in eggs and vanilla. Add combined dry ingredients alternately with milk, mixing well after each addition. Pour batter into greased and floured 13 × 9-inch baking pan. Sprinkle with nut mixture. Bake at 350°, 30 minutes or until wooden pick inserted in center comes out clean.

12 servings

CREAMY ORANGE RINGS

1 8-ounce package PHILADELPHIA BRAND
   Cream Cheese, softened
1/2 cup granulated sugar
1 tablespoon grated orange peel
2 8-ounce cans PILLSBURY Refrigerated
   Quick Crescent Dinner Rolls
1/3 cup chopped almonds

* * *

1/2 cup powdered sugar
1 tablespoon orange juice

Combine cream cheese, granulated sugar and peel, mixing until well blended. For each can of rolls, unroll dough onto lightly floured surface. Overlap long edges of rectangles to form 13 × 7-inch rectangle, pressing edges together to seal. Spread rectangle with half of cream cheese mixture; sprinkle with half of almonds. Roll up dough starting at long side, pressing edges together to seal. Shape into ring, seam-side down, on greased cookie sheet. Press ends together to seal. Cut two-thirds through ring from outer edge at 1-inch intervals, leaving center of ring intact. Turn each section on its side. Bake at 375°, 15 minutes.

Combine powdered sugar and juice; drizzle on warm coffeecake rings. Garnish with maraschino cherry halves and additional almonds, sliced, if desired.

12 servings

Creamy Orange Ring ▶

KOLACHY

4¹/₂ to 4³/₄ cups flour
¹/₂ cup sugar
2 packages active dry yeast
1 teaspoon salt
³/₄ cup milk
¹/₂ cup PARKAY Margarine
3 eggs
¹/₂ teaspoon grated lemon peel
Cream Cheese Filling or Prune Filling

In large mixing bowl, combine 1 cup flour, sugar, yeast and salt. Heat milk and margarine over low heat until warm. Add to flour mixture; beat 3 minutes at medium speed on electric mixer. Add ¹/₂ cup flour, eggs and peel; beat 2 minutes at high speed. Stir in enough remaining flour to form soft dough. On lightly floured surface, knead dough until smooth and elastic, about 5 minutes. Place in greased bowl; brush with additional margarine, melted. Cover; let rise in warm place until double in volume, about 1¹/₂ hours. Punch down dough; divide in half. Cover; let rest 10 minutes. Shape each half into twelve balls. Place 3 inches apart on greased cookie sheet; flatten to 3-inch circles. Cover; let rise until double in volume, about 45 minutes. Indent centers; fill with measuring tablespoonfuls of Cream Cheese Filling or Prune Filling. Bake at 375°, 8 to 10 minutes or until golden brown. Remove from cookie sheet; sprinkle with sifted powdered sugar, if desired.   *2 dozen*

CREAM CHEESE FILLING

1 8-ounce package PHILADELPHIA BRAND
  Cream Cheese, softened
¹/₄ cup sugar
1 egg
¹/₄ teaspoon grated orange peel

Combine cream cheese and remaining ingredients, mixing until well blended.

PRUNE FILLING

2 cups dried pitted prunes
¹/₃ cup sugar
2 teaspoons lemon juice
¹/₂ teaspoon cinnamon

Cover prunes with water; bring to boil. Boil 10 minutes. Drain; chop. Combine prunes and remaining ingredients; mix well.

CHOCOLATE CHIP STREUSEL COFFEECAKE

¹/₂ cup packed brown sugar
¹/₂ cup flour
¹/₄ cup PARKAY Margarine
¹/₄ cup chopped walnuts
1 cup mini semi-sweet chocolate pieces

* * *

1 8-ounce package PHILADELPHIA BRAND Cream Cheese, softened
1¹/₂ cups granulated sugar
³/₄ cup PARKAY Margarine
3 eggs, beaten
³/₄ teaspoon vanilla
2¹/₂ cups flour
1¹/₂ teaspoons baking powder
³/₄ teaspoon baking soda
¹/₄ teaspoon salt
³/₄ cup milk

Combine brown sugar and flour; cut in margarine until mixture resembles coarse crumbs. Stir in walnuts and chocolate pieces.

Combine cream cheese, granulated sugar and margarine, mixing at medium speed on electric mixer until well blended. Blend in eggs and vanilla. Add combined dry ingredients alternately with milk, mixing well after each addition. Spoon batter into greased and floured 13 × 9-inch baking pan. Sprinkle with crumb mixture. Bake at 350°, 50 minutes or until wooden pick inserted in center comes out clean. Cool.

12 to 16 servings

VARIATION

■ Substitute loose bottom 10-inch tube pan for 13 × 9-inch baking pan. Bake at 350°, 1 hour or until wooden pick inserted in center comes out clean. Cool 10 minutes; remove tube insert from outer pan. Cool thoroughly before removing cake from tube insert.

BLUEBERRIES 'N CHEESE COFFEECAKE

1/2 cup PARKAY Margarine
1 1/4 cups granulated sugar
2 eggs
2 1/4 cups flour
1 tablespoon baking powder
1 teaspoon salt
3/4 cup milk
1/4 cup water
2 cups blueberries
1 8-ounce package PHILADELPHIA BRAND
   Cream Cheese, cubed
1 teaspoon grated lemon peel

*   *   *

1/4 cup granulated sugar
1/4 cup flour
1 teaspoon grated lemon peel
2 tablespoons PARKAY Margarine
   Powdered sugar

Beat margarine and granulated sugar until light and fluffy. Add eggs, one at a time, mixing well after each addition. Add combined 2 cups flour, baking powder and salt alternately with combined milk and water, mixing well after each addition. Toss blueberries with remaining flour; fold into batter with cream cheese and peel. Pour into greased and floured 13 × 9-inch baking pan.

Combine granulated sugar, flour and peel; cut in margarine until mixture resembles coarse crumbs. Sprinkle over batter. Bake at 375°, 1 hour. Cool. Sprinkle with powdered sugar before serving.

12 servings

VARIATION
■ Substitute 2 cups frozen blueberries, thawed, well-drained, for fresh blueberries.

CRANBERRY MUFFINS AND CREAMY ORANGE SPREAD

    2 cups flour
    6 tablespoons sugar
    2 teaspoons baking powder
 $1/2$ teaspoon salt
 $3/4$ cup milk
 $1/2$ cup PARKAY Margarine, melted
    1 egg, beaten
 $3/4$ cup coarsely chopped cranberries

                 *   *   *

    1 8-ounce package PHILADELPHIA BRAND
         Cream Cheese, softened
    1 tablespoon sugar
    1 tablespoon orange juice
    1 teaspoon grated orange peel

Combine flour, 4 tablespoons sugar, baking powder and salt; mix well. Add combined milk, margarine and egg, mixing just until moistened. Fold in combined remaining sugar and cranberries. Spoon into greased medium-size muffin pan, filling each cup $2/3$ full. Bake at 400°, 20 to 25 minutes or until golden brown.

Combine cream cheese, sugar, orange juice and peel, mixing until well blended. Chill. Serve with muffins.

1 dozen

VARIATION
■ Substitute *Light* PHILADELPHIA BRAND Neufchâtel Cheese for Cream Cheese.

DESSERT DISCOVERIES

FESTIVE CRANBERRY TORTE

1 8-ounce package PHILADELPHIA BRAND
  Cream Cheese, softened
1/4 cup sugar
1/2 cup whipping cream, whipped
1 10 3/4-ounce frozen pound cake, thawed
1 14-ounce jar cranberry orange sauce

Combine cream cheese and sugar, mixing until well blended. Fold in whipped cream. Split cake horizontally into four layers. Spread bottom layer with 1/2 cup cranberry orange sauce; top with second layer. Spread second layer with 2/3 cup cream cheese mixture; top with third layer. Spread third layer with 1/2 cup cranberry orange sauce. Cover with top cake layer. Frost top and sides of torte with remaining cream cheese mixture. Chill several hours or overnight. Top with remaining cranberry orange sauce just before serving. Garnish with whole cranberries and fresh mint, if desired.

10 to 12 servings

VARIATION
■ Substitute *Light* PHILADELPHIA BRAND Neufchâtel Cheese for Cream Cheese.

CHOCOLATEY PEANUT TREATS

1 8-ounce container Soft PHILADELPHIA
  BRAND Cream Cheese
1/2 cup peanut butter
1 6-ounce package semi-sweet chocolate
  pieces, melted
2 1/4 cups graham cracker crumbs
2/3 cup finely chopped peanuts

Combine cream cheese and peanut butter, mixing until well blended. Blend in chocolate. Stir in graham cracker crumbs; mix well. Shape into 1-inch balls. Roll in peanuts; chill.

4 dozen

VARIATION
■ Omit peanuts. Prepare, shape and chill dough as directed. Roll in powdered sugar just before serving.

◄ *Festive Cranberry Torte*

CHOCOLATE ALMOND "PHILLY" TORTE

1 8-ounce package PHILADELPHIA BRAND
 Cream Cheese, softened
¼ cup PARKAY Margarine
1 cup sugar
2 eggs
½ teaspoon vanilla
1½ cups flour
1 teaspoon baking soda
½ teaspoon baking powder
½ cup milk
2 1-ounce squares unsweetened chocolate,
 melted
 Almond and Chocolate "Philly" Cream
 Frostings

Combine cream cheese, margarine and sugar, mixing until well blended. Blend in eggs and vanilla. Add combined dry ingredients alternately with milk, mixing well after each addition. Blend in chocolate. Spread batter evenly into wax paper-lined 15 × 10 × 1-inch jelly roll pan. Bake at 350°, 12 to 15 minutes or until wooden pick inserted in center comes out clean. Cool thoroughly. Cut crosswise into four equal sections; remove from pan. Spread three sections with almond frosting; chill until frosting is firm. Stack. Top with remaining layer; frost top and sides with chocolate frosting. *12 servings*

ALMOND AND CHOCOLATE "PHILLY" CREAM FROSTINGS

1 8-ounce package PHILADELPHIA BRAND
 Cream Cheese, softened
6½ cups sifted powdered sugar
½ cup whipping cream
½ cup chopped almonds, toasted
2 1-ounce squares unsweetened chocolate,
 melted

Beat cream cheese at medium speed on electric mixer. Gradually add 5 cups sugar, mixing well after each addition. Add whipping cream, beating at high speed until creamy. Divide mixture in half. Add remaining sugar and almonds to one half, mixing until well blended. Stir chocolate into remaining half. Chill chocolate frosting until thickened for spreading consistency.

"Philly" Fruit Clouds

"PHILLY" FRUIT CLOUDS

> 1 8-ounce package PHILADELPHIA BRAND
>   Cream Cheese, softened
> 1/2 cup sugar
> 1 tablespoon lemon juice
> 2 teaspoons grated lemon peel
> 1 cup whipping cream, whipped
>   Assorted fruit

Combine cream cheese, sugar, juice and peel, mixing until well blended. Fold in whipped cream. With back of spoon, shape on wax paper-lined cookie sheet to form ten shells; freeze. Fill each shell with fruit. Garnish with fresh mint, if desired.

10 servings

VARIATIONS
■ Prepare cream cheese mixture as directed. Spread into 8-inch square pan; freeze. Cut into squares; top with fruit.
■ Substitute *Light* PHILADELPHIA BRAND Neufchâtel Cheese for Cream Cheese.

"PHILLY" APRICOT COOKIES

1½ cups PARKAY Margarine
1½ cups granulated sugar
1 8-ounce package PHILADELPHIA BRAND
    Cream Cheese, softened
2 eggs
2 tablespoons lemon juice
1½ teaspoons grated lemon peel
4½ cups flour
1½ teaspoons baking powder
    KRAFT Apricot Preserves
    Powdered sugar

Combine margarine, granulated sugar and cream cheese, mixing until well blended. Blend in eggs, juice and peel. Add combined flour and baking powder; mix well. Chill several hours. Shape level measuring tablespoonfuls of dough into balls. Place on ungreased cookie sheet; flatten slightly. Indent centers; fill with preserves. Bake at 350°, 15 minutes. Cool; sprinkle with powdered sugar.

Approximately 7 dozen

"PHILLY" BANANA PUDDING

12 vanilla wafers
1 8-ounce container Soft PHILADELPHIA
    BRAND Cream Cheese
2 tablespoons milk
2 tablespoons sugar
1 teaspoon vanilla
2 cups thawed frozen whipped topping
2 medium bananas, sliced

Line bottom and sides of 1-quart serving bowl with wafers. Combine cream cheese, milk, sugar and vanilla, mixing until well blended. Fold in remaining ingredients. Spoon into bowl; chill.

6 servings

Top: Pecan Tassies (see page 110)
Center: Chocolate "Philly" Fudge (see page 110)
Bottom: "Philly" Apricot Cookies ▶

CHOCOLATE "PHILLY" FUDGE

    4 cups sifted powdered sugar
    1 8-ounce package PHILADELPHIA BRAND
        Cream Cheese, softened
    4 1-ounce squares unsweetened chocolate,
        melted
    1 teaspoon vanilla
        Dash of salt
    ½ cup chopped nuts

Gradually add sugar to cream cheese, mixing well after each addition. Add remaining ingredients; mix well. Spread into greased 8-inch square pan. Chill several hours; cut into squares.

1¾ pounds

VARIATIONS
■ Omit vanilla and nuts; add few drops peppermint extract and ¼ cup crushed peppermint candy. Sprinkle with additional ¼ cup crushed peppermint candy before chilling.
■ Omit nuts; add 1 cup shredded coconut. Garnish with additional coconut.
■ Omit nuts; add ½ cup chopped maraschino cherries, drained. Garnish with whole cherries.

PECAN TASSIES

    1 8-ounce package PHILADELPHIA BRAND
        Cream Cheese, softened
    1 cup PARKAY Margarine
    2 cups flour
    2 eggs, beaten
    1½ cups packed brown sugar
    2 teaspoons vanilla
    1½ cups chopped pecans

Combine cream cheese and margarine, mixing until well blended. Add flour; mix well. Chill. Divide dough into quarters; divide each quarter into 12 balls. Press each ball onto bottom and sides of miniature muffin pans. Combine eggs, brown sugar and vanilla; stir in pecans. Spoon into pastry shells, filling each cup. Bake at 325°, 30 minutes or until pastry is golden brown. Cool 5 minutes; remove from pans. Sprinkle with powdered sugar, if desired.

4 dozen

CHERRY 'N OAT SQUARES

1¼ cups old fashioned or quick oats, uncooked
⅓ cup PARKAY Margarine, melted
¼ cup sugar

*   *   *

1 8-ounce package PHILADELPHIA BRAND
   Cream Cheese, softened
¼ cup sugar
1 egg
1 21-ounce can cherry pie filling

Combine oats, margarine and sugar; press onto bottom of greased 8-inch square pan. Bake at 400°, 15 minutes.

Combine cream cheese and sugar, mixing at medium speed on electric mixer until well blended. Blend in egg. Pour over crust. Bake at 350°, 10 to 15 minutes or until set. Spread pie filling over cream cheese mixture; continue baking 15 minutes. Chill.

8 servings

ACAPULCO FLAN

20 KRAFT Caramels
2 tablespoons water
1 8-ounce package PHILADELPHIA BRAND
   Cream Cheese, softened
½ cup sugar
6 eggs, beaten
1 teaspoon vanilla
2 cups milk

Melt caramels with water over low heat, stirring until smooth. Pour into greased 9-inch layer pan. Combine cream cheese and sugar, mixing until well blended. Blend in eggs and vanilla. Gradually add milk, mixing until well blended. Set layer pan in baking pan on oven rack; slowly pour milk mixture over caramel sauce. Pour boiling water into baking pan to ½-inch depth. Bake at 350°, 45 minutes or until knife inserted 2-inches from edge of pan comes out clean. Remove from water immediately; cool 5 minutes. Invert onto serving dish with rim. Serve warm or chilled.

6 to 8 servings

SURPRISE CARROT CAKE

1 8-ounce package PHILADELPHIA BRAND
Cream Cheese, softened

1/4 cup sugar

1 egg, beaten

*　　*　　*

2 cups flour

1 3/4 cups sugar

2 teaspoons baking soda

2 teaspoons cinnamon

1 teaspoon salt

1 cup oil

3 eggs, beaten

3 cups shredded carrot

1/2 cup chopped nuts

Combine cream cheese, sugar and egg, mixing until well blended. Set aside.

Combine dry ingredients. Add combined oil and eggs, mixing just until moistened. Fold in carrots and nuts. Reserve 2 cups batter; pour remaining batter into greased and floured 9-inch bundt pan. Pour cream cheese mixture over batter; carefully spoon reserved batter over cream cheese mixture, spreading to cover. Bake at 350°, 55 minutes or until wooden pick inserted in center comes out clean. Cool 10 minutes; remove from pan. Cool thoroughly. Sprinkle with powdered sugar, if desired.

12 servings

VARIATION
■ Substitute *Light* PHILADELPHIA BRAND Neufchâtel
Cheese for Cream Cheese.

◄ *Surprise Carrot Cake*

HOT FRUIT COMPOTE

1 20-ounce can pineapple chunks, drained
1 17-ounce can apricot halves, drained
1 16-ounce can pitted dark sweet cherries,
    drained
¼ cup packed brown sugar
½ teaspoon ground nutmeg
¼ cup PARKAY Margarine
    Soft PHILADELPHIA BRAND Cream
    Cheese

Combine fruit in 1½-quart casserole. Sprinkle with combined sugar and nutmeg; dot with margarine. Bake at 350°, 20 minutes. Serve warm with cream cheese.   *6 to 8 servings*

VARIATION
■ Substitute curry powder for nutmeg.

MICROWAVE
Prepare as directed. Microwave on High 5 minutes, stirring every 2 minutes. Stir before serving. Serve as directed.

TORTONI SQUARES

1 envelope unflavored gelatin
½ cup cold water
2 8-ounce containers Soft PHILADELPHIA
    BRAND Cream Cheese
2 tablespoons sugar
1 17-ounce can apricot halves, drained,
    chopped
2 tablespoons chopped almonds, toasted
¼ teaspoon rum flavoring
2 cups thawed frozen whipped topping
2 cups macaroon cookies, crumbled

Soften gelatin in water; stir over low heat until dissolved. Cool. Combine cream cheese and sugar, mixing until well blended. Gradually add gelatin, mixing until blended. Stir in apricots, almonds and flavoring. Fold in whipped topping. Place macaroons on bottom of 9-inch square baking pan; top with cream cheese mixture. Chill; cut into squares.

9 servings

Peach Surprise Pie

PEACH SURPRISE PIE

2 8-ounce packages *Light* PHILADELPHIA
   BRAND Neufchâtel Cheese, softened
1/4 cup sugar
1/2 teaspoon vanilla
   Pastry for 1-crust 9-inch pie, baked
1 16-ounce can peach slices, drained
1/4 cup KRAFT Red Raspberry Preserves
1 teaspoon lemon juice

Combine neufchâtel cheese, sugar and vanilla, mixing until well blended. Spread onto bottom of crust; chill several hours or overnight. Top with peaches just before serving. Combine preserves and juice, mixing until well blended. Spoon over peaches. Garnish with fresh mint, if desired.

6 to 8 servings

"PHILLY" CHOCOLATE SAUCE

    1 8-ounce package PHILADELPHIA BRAND
        Cream Cheese, cubed
  1/3 cup milk
    2 1-ounce squares unsweetened chocolate
    2 cups sifted powdered sugar
    1 teaspoon vanilla

Combine cream cheese, milk and chocolate; stir over low heat until smooth. Blend in remaining ingredients. Serve over poached pears, ice cream or cake.

2 cups

NOTE
This sauce can be refrigerated and then reheated.

FROSTY ORANGE DESSERT

    1 3-ounce package orange flavored gelatin
    1 cup boiling water
  1/2 cup cold water
  1/3 cup orange juice
    1 teaspoon grated orange peel
    1 8-ounce package *Light* PHILADELPHIA
        BRAND Neufchâtel Cheese, softened
  1/4 cup sugar

Dissolve gelatin in boiling water; add cold water, juice and peel. Combine neufchâtel cheese and sugar, mixing until well blended. Gradually add gelatin mixture to neufchâtel cheese mixture, mixing until blended. Chill, stirring occasionally, until thickened but not set. Beat with electric mixer until fluffy. Spoon into individual parfait glasses; chill several hours or overnight.

6 to 8 servings

VARIATIONS
■ Substitute PHILADELPHIA BRAND Cream Cheese for Neufchâtel Cheese.
■ Substitute lime flavored gelatin for orange flavored gelatin. Reduce orange juice to 1/4 cup. Add 2 tablespoons lime juice with orange juice. Substitute lime peel for orange peel.

"Philly" Chocolate Sauce ▶

KANSAS CITY PIE

1¹/₄ cups finely chopped pecans

³/₄ cup flour

¹/₄ cup PARKAY Margarine, melted

*   *   *

2 8-ounce packages PHILADELPHIA BRAND
    Cream Cheese, softened

1¹/₂ cups powdered sugar

1 8-ounce container (3 cups) frozen whipped
    topping, thawed

2 4-ounce packages chocolate instant
    pudding and pie filling mix

2²/₃ cups milk

Combine pecans, flour and margarine; press onto bottom of 9-inch springform pan. Bake at 375°, 20 minutes. Cool.

Combine cream cheese and sugar, mixing until well blended. Fold in 1¹/₂ cups whipped topping; spread over crust. Prepare mix as directed on package for pudding, except using 2²/₃ cups milk. Spoon over cream cheese layer. Chill several hours or overnight. Loosen pie from rim of pan; remove rim of pan. Spread remaining whipped topping over pudding layer just before serving.

10 to 12 servings

TOASTED ALMOND SOUFFLE

1 8-ounce package PHILADELPHIA BRAND
    Cream Cheese, softened

¹/₃ cup sugar

¹/₂ teaspoon almond extract

¹/₄ teaspoon salt

4 eggs, separated

¹/₂ cup half and half

2 tablespoons sliced almonds

Combine cream cheese, sugar, extract and salt, mixing until well blended. Lightly beat egg yolks; blend into cream cheese mixture. Gradually add half and half. Beat egg whites until stiff peaks form. Fold into cream cheese mixture; pour into 1¹/₂-quart souffle dish. With tip of spoon, make slight indentation or "track" around top of souffle 1-inch from edge to form top hat. Top with almonds. Bake at 325°, 50 minutes or until light golden brown.

6 to 8 servings

BAVARIAN LEMON CREME

1 envelope unflavored gelatin
1/2 cup cold water
2 8-ounce packages *Light* PHILADELPHIA
    BRAND Neufchâtel Cheese, softened
1/3 cup sugar
1/4 cup milk
1/4 cup lemon juice
1/2 teaspoon grated lemon peel
2 egg whites
2 cups thawed frozen whipped topping
   Lemon Sauce

Soften gelatin in water; stir over low heat until dissolved. Combine neufchâtel cheese and sugar, mixing until well blended. Gradually add gelatin, milk, juice and peel, mixing until blended. Chill, stirring occasionally, until thickened but not set. Beat with electric mixer or wire whisk until smooth. Beat egg whites until stiff peaks form. Fold egg whites and whipped topping into neufchâtel cheese mixture. Pour into lightly oiled 1 1/2-quart mold; chill until firm. Unmold; serve with Lemon Sauce.

8 to 10 servings

LEMON SAUCE

3/4 cup sugar
2 tablespoons cornstarch
1/4 cup water
1/4 cup lemon juice
2 egg yolks, beaten

Combine sugar and cornstarch in saucepan; gradually add water and juice. Cook, stirring constantly, until mixture is clear and thickened. Stir small amount of hot mixture into egg yolks; return to hot mixture. Cook, stirring constantly, over low heat until thickened. Cool.

VARIATION
■ Substitute PHILADELPHIA BRAND Cream Cheese for Neufchâtel Cheese. Increase sugar to 1/2 cup. Substitute 1 cup whipping cream, whipped, for whipped topping.

STRAWBERRY TART GLACE

Pastry for 1-crust 9-inch pie

* * *

2 8-ounce packages *Light* **PHILADELPHIA BRAND Neufchâtel Cheese, softened**

1/2 cup sugar

1 tablespoon milk

1/4 teaspoon vanilla

1 quart strawberries, hulled

1 tablespoon cornstarch

1/4 cup water

Few drops red food coloring (optional)

On lightly floured surface, roll pastry to 12-inch circle. Place in 10-inch quiche dish. Prick bottom and sides of pastry with fork. Bake at 450°, 9 to 11 minutes or until golden brown.

Combine neufchâtel cheese, 1/4 cup sugar, milk and vanilla, mixing at medium speed on electric mixer until well blended. Spread onto bottom of crust. Puree 1 cup strawberries. Top neufchâtel cheese mixture with remaining strawberries. Combine remaining sugar and cornstarch in saucepan; gradually add pureed strawberries and water. Cook, stirring constantly, over medium heat until mixture is clear and thickened. Stir in food coloring. Pour over strawberries; chill.

8 servings

VARIATIONS

▪ Substitute 9-inch pie plate for 10-inch quiche dish.

▪ Substitute almond extract for vanilla.

▪ Substitute PHILADELPHIA BRAND Cream Cheese for Neufchâtel Cheese.

Strawberry Tart Glace ▶

Marble Squares

MARBLE SQUARES

$^1/_2$ cup PARKAY Margarine

$^3/_4$ cup water

$1^1/_2$ 1-ounce squares unsweetened chocolate

2 cups flour

2 cups sugar

1 teaspoon baking soda

$^1/_2$ teaspoon salt

2 eggs, beaten

$^1/_2$ cup sour cream

* * *

1 8-ounce package PHILADELPHIA BRAND
Cream Cheese, softened

$^1/_3$ cup sugar

1 egg

1 6-ounce package semi-sweet chocolate
pieces

(continued)

Combine margarine, water and chocolate in saucepan; bring to boil. Remove from heat. Stir in combined flour, sugar, baking soda and salt. Add eggs and sour cream; mix well. Pour into greased and floured 15 × 10 × 1-inch jelly roll pan.

Combine cream cheese and sugar, mixing until well blended. Blend in egg. Spoon over chocolate batter. Cut through batter with knife several times for marble effect. Sprinkle with chocolate pieces. Bake at 375°, 25 to 30 minutes or until wooden pick inserted in center comes out clean.

Approximately 2 dozen

PARADISE PUMPKIN PIE

Pastry for 1-crust 9-inch pie

1 8-ounce package PHILADELPHIA BRAND
Cream Cheese, softened

1/4 cup sugar

1/2 teaspoon vanilla

1 egg

*   *   *

1 1/4 cups canned pumpkin

1 cup evaporated milk

1/2 cup sugar

2 eggs, beaten

1 teaspoon cinnamon

1/4 teaspoon ground ginger

1/4 teaspoon ground nutmeg

Dash of salt

Maple syrup

Pecan halves

On lightly floured surface, roll pastry to 12-inch circle. Place in 9-inch pie plate. Turn under edge; flute. Combine cream cheese, sugar and vanilla, mixing at medium speed on electric mixer until well blended. Blend in egg. Spread onto bottom of pastry shell.

Combine all remaining ingredients except syrup and pecans; mix well. Carefully pour over cream cheese mixture. Bake at 350°, 65 minutes. Cool. Brush with syrup; top with pecans.

8 servings

PINEAPPLE "PHILLY" PIE

Pastry for 1-crust 9-inch pie

$^1/_3$ cup sugar

1 tablespoon cornstarch

1 8$^1/_4$-ounce can crushed pineapple,
  undrained

* * *

1 8-ounce package PHILADELPHIA BRAND
  Cream Cheese, softened

$^1/_2$ cup sugar

$^1/_2$ teaspoon salt

2 eggs

$^1/_2$ cup milk

$^1/_2$ teaspoon vanilla

$^1/_4$ cup chopped pecans

On lightly floured surface, roll pastry to 12-inch circle. Place in 9-inch pie plate. Turn under edge; flute. Combine sugar and cornstarch in saucepan; stir in pineapple. Cook, stirring constantly, until mixture is clear and thickened. Cool; spread onto bottom of pastry shell.

Combine cream cheese, sugar and salt, mixing until well blended. Add eggs, one at a time, mixing well after each addition. Blend in milk and vanilla. Pour over pineapple mixture; sprinkle with pecans. Bake at 350°, 35 minutes. Cool. Garnish with pineapple slices, cut in half, and maraschino cherry halves, if desired.

8 servings

Top: Creme de Menthe Pie (see page 126)
Center: Pineapple "Philly" Pie
Bottom: Paradise Pumpkin Pie (see page 123) ▶

CREME DE MENTHE PIE

2 cups (24) crushed creme-filled chocolate
    cookies
¼ cup PARKAY Margarine, melted

        *   *   *

2 8-ounce packages PHILADELPHIA BRAND
    Cream Cheese, softened
1½ cups sifted powdered sugar
2 tablespoons green creme de menthe
2 cups whipping cream, whipped

Combine crumbs and margarine; press onto bottom and sides of 9-inch pie plate.

Combine cream cheese, sugar and creme de menthe, mixing until well blended. Fold in whipped cream; pour into crust. Chill several hours or overnight. Garnish with chocolate curls, if desired.

8 servings

RASPBERRY FREEZE

¼ cup honey
1 8-ounce package PHILADELPHIA BRAND
    Cream Cheese, softened
1 10-ounce package frozen raspberries,
    partially thawed, undrained
1 cup banana slices
2 cups KRAFT Miniature Marshmallows
1 cup whipping cream, whipped

Gradually add honey to cream cheese, mixing until well blended. Stir in fruit; fold in marshmallows and whipped cream. Pour into lightly oiled 9-inch square pan; freeze. Place in refrigerator 30 minutes before serving. Cut into squares.

9 servings

VARIATIONS

■ Prepare as directed. Spoon raspberry mixture into ten 5-ounce paper drinking cups; insert wooden sticks in center. Freeze.

■ Prepare as directed. Pour raspberry mixture into lightly oiled 9-inch springform pan with ring insert; freeze. Place in refrigerator 1 hour before serving. Loosen dessert from rim of pan; remove rim of pan.

Favorite Layer Bars

FAVORITE LAYER BARS

1¹/₂ cups graham cracker crumbs

¹/₄ cup sugar

¹/₄ cup PARKAY Margarine, melted

*   *   *

1 8-ounce package PHILADELPHIA BRAND
Cream Cheese, softened

¹/₂ cup sugar

1 egg

³/₄ cup flaked coconut

³/₄ cup chopped nuts

1 6-ounce package semi-sweet chocolate
pieces

Combine crumbs, sugar and margarine; press onto bottom of 13 × 9-inch baking pan. Bake at 325°, 10 minutes.

Combine cream cheese, sugar and egg, mixing until well blended. Spread over crust. Sprinkle with combined coconut, nuts and chocolate pieces; press lightly into surface. Bake at 350°, 25 to 30 minutes or until lightly browned. Cool; cut into bars.

Approximately 3 dozen

FRUIT PIZZA

1 20-ounce package PILLSBURY'S BEST
  Refrigerated Sugar Cookies

*   *   *

1 8-ounce package PHILADELPHIA BRAND
  Cream Cheese, softened
1/3 cup sugar
1/2 teaspoon vanilla
  Banana slices
  Peeled kiwi slices
  Strawberry halves
  Blueberries
1/2 cup KRAFT Orange Marmalade, Peach or
  Apricot Preserves
2 tablespoons water

Freeze cookie dough 1 hour. Slice into 1/8-inch slices. Line foil-lined 14-inch pizza pan with slices, overlapping edges slightly. Bake at 375°, 12 minutes or until golden brown. Cool. Invert onto serving plate; carefully remove foil. Invert to right side.

Combine cream cheese, sugar and vanilla, mixing until well blended. Spread over crust. Arrange fruit over cream cheese layer. Glaze with combined marmalade and water; chill. Cut into wedges.

10 to 12 servings

VARIATIONS
■ Substitute Soft PHILADELPHIA BRAND Cream Cheese for regular Cream Cheese.
■ Substitute one or more of the following for the banana, kiwi, strawberries and blueberries:
  Raspberries
  Red or green grape halves
  Pineapple chunks
  Maraschino cherry halves, drained
  Thin sliced peaches, pears or apples
  Mandarin orange segments, drainged

TIP
Arrange fruit to create a variety of shapes and designs—try stripes, triangles or circles.

Fruit Pizza▶

SNOW TOPPED APPLES

2 medium baking apples
2 teaspoons raisins
2 teaspoons chopped nuts
Dash of cinnamon
2 teaspoons PARKAY Margarine
2 tablespoons *Light* PHILADELPHIA
     BRAND Neufchâtel Cheese

Core apples; remove peel around top of apples. Place each in 10-ounce custard cup. Fill center of apples with combined raisins, nuts and cinnamon; dot with margarine. Bake at 375°, 25 to 30 minutes or until soft. Top warm apples with neufchâtel cheese. Sprinkle with additional chopped nuts, if desired.

2 servings

VARIATION
■ Substitute Soft PHILADELPHIA BRAND Cream Cheese for Neufchâtel Cheese.

MICROWAVE
Prepare apples as directed. Cover custard cups with plastic wrap vented at one edge. Microwave on High 2½ to 3 minutes or until apples are soft. Serve as directed.

SUNRISE CHERRY PIE

1 8¼-ounce can crushed pineapple,
     undrained
1 8-ounce package PHILADELPHIA BRAND
     Cream Cheese, softened
½ teaspoon vanilla
1 21-ounce can cherry pie filling
¼ cup powdered sugar
1 cup whipping cream
1 9-inch graham cracker crumb crust

Drain pineapple well, reserving two tablespoons liquid. Combine reserved liquid, cream cheese and vanilla, mixing until well blended. Stir in ¼ cup pineapple and ½ cup pie filling. Gradually add sugar to cream, beating until soft peaks form. Fold into cream cheese mixture; pour into crust. Top with remaining pineapple and pie filling. Chill until firm.

6 to 8 servings

CARAMEL PECAN PIE

Pastry for 1-crust 9-inch pie
36 KRAFT Caramels
1/4 cup PARKAY Margarine
1/4 cup water
3/4 cup sugar
3 eggs, beaten
1/2 teaspoon vanilla
1/4 teaspoon salt
1 cup pecan halves

On lightly floured surface, roll pastry to 12-inch circle. Place in 9-inch pie plate. Turn under edge; flute. Melt caramels and margarine with water in heavy saucepan over low heat, stirring frequently until smooth. Gradually add to combined sugar, eggs, vanilla and salt; mix well. Stir in pecans; pour into pastry shell. Bake at 350°, 45 to 50 minutes or until pastry is golden brown. Cool. (Filling appears soft, but will firm as it cools.)

8 servings

VARIATION
■ Substitute cashews, chopped walnuts or peanuts for pecan halves.

CREAMY RICE DESSERT

1 8 1/4-ounce can crushed pineapple, undrained
2 cups cooked rice, chilled
1 11-ounce can mandarin orange segments, drained
1/2 cup maraschino cherry halves
1/2 cup chopped nuts
1 8-ounce container Soft PHILADELPHIA BRAND Cream Cheese
1/4 cup sugar
1/4 teaspoon vanilla

Drain pineapple, reserving 3 tablespoons liquid. Combine pineapple, rice, orange segments, cherries and nuts; mix lightly. Combine reserved liquid, cream cheese, sugar and vanilla, mixing until well blended. Add to rice mixture; mix lightly.

6 servings

Raspberry Fudge Balls

1 8-ounce package PHILADELPHIA BRAND
   Cream Cheese, softened
1 6-ounce package semi-sweet chocolate
   pieces, melted
3/4 cup vanilla wafer crumbs
1/4 cup KRAFT Raspberry Preserves, strained
   Finely chopped almonds
   Cocoa
   Powdered sugar

Combine cream cheese and chocolate, mixing until well blended. Stir in crumbs and preserves. Chill several hours or overnight. Shape into 1-inch balls; roll in almonds, cocoa or sugar.

Approximately 3 dozen

Minty Chocolate Squares

1 6-ounce package semi-sweet chocolate
   pieces
1 cup PARKAY Margarine
1 3/4 cups graham cracker crumbs
1 cup flaked coconut
1/2 cup chopped nuts
2 8-ounce packages PHILADELPHIA BRAND
   Cream Cheese, softened
1 cup sifted powdered sugar
1/2 teaspoon mint extract
   Few drops green food coloring (optional)

Melt 1/3 cup chocolate pieces with 3/4 cup margarine over low heat, stirring until smooth. Add combined crumbs, coconut and nuts; mix well. Press onto bottom of ungreased 13 × 9-inch baking pan; chill. Combine cream cheese, sugar, extract and food coloring, mixing until well blended. Spread over crust; chill. Melt remaining chocolate pieces with remaining margarine over low heat, stirring until smooth. Spread over cream cheese layer; chill. Cut into squares. Serve chilled.

Approximately 3 dozen

◄ *Raspberry Fudge Balls*

"PHILLY" CREAM PUFF RING

1 cup water
1/2 cup PARKAY Margarine
1 cup flour
1/4 teaspoon salt
4 eggs

*　　*　　*

2 8-ounce packages PHILADELPHIA BRAND
　Cream Cheese, softened
1 1/2 cups powdered sugar
1 teaspoon vanilla
1 cup whipping cream, whipped
2 bananas, sliced
1 1-ounce square unsweetened chocolate,
　melted
1 tablespoon milk

Bring water and margarine to boil. Add flour and salt; stir vigorously over low heat until mixture forms ball. Remove from heat. Add eggs, one at a time, beating well after each addition. Drop ten 1/2 cupfuls of dough on lightly greased cookie sheet to form 9-inch ring. Bake at 400°, 50 to 55 minutes or until golden brown. Remove from cookie sheet immediately; cool.

Combine cream cheese, 1 cup sugar and vanilla, mixing until well blended. Reserve 1/2 cup cream cheese mixture; fold whipped cream and bananas into remaining mixture. Chill. Carefully cut top from ring; fill with whipped cream mixture. Replace top. Add remaining sugar, chocolate and milk to reserved cream cheese mixture; mix well. Spread over ring.

10 servings

"Philly" Cream Puff Ring ▶

"Philly" Frosted Cookies

"PHILLY" FROSTED COOKIES

Oatmeal cookies or chocolate chip cookies
Soft PHILADELPHIA BRAND Cream
  Cheese
Peeled kiwi slices
Mandarin orange segments
Strawberry slices

For each serving, spread cookie with cream cheese; top with remaining ingredients as desired.

VARIATION
■ Substitute Soft PHILADELPHIA BRAND Cream Cheese
with Strawberries for Soft Cream Cheese.

GERMAN APPLE TORTE

1/3 cup PARKAY Margarine

1/3 cup sugar

1 egg

1 1/4 cups flour

* * *

2 8-ounce packages *Light* PHILADELPHIA
   BRAND Neufchâtel Cheese, softened

1/2 cup sugar

2 tablespoons flour

1/2 teaspoon vanilla

2 eggs

1 1/4 cups peeled chopped apple

1/4 cup sliced almonds

1/3 cup KRAFT Grape or Red Currant Jelly,
   heated

Beat margarine and sugar until light and fluffy. Blend in egg. Add flour; mix well. Spread dough onto bottom and 1 1/4-inches up sides of 9-inch springform pan. Bake at 425°, 5 to 7 minutes or until crust is lightly browned.

Combine neufchâtel cheese, sugar, flour and vanilla, mixing at medium speed on electric mixer until well blended. Add eggs, one at a time, mixing well after each addition. Pour into crust. Top with apples and almonds. Bake at 425°, 10 minutes. Reduce oven temperature to 350°; continue baking 30 minutes. Drizzle with jelly. Loosen cake from rim of pan; cool before removing rim of pan. Chill several hours or overnight.

10 to 12 servings

CHERRY NUT CAKE

1 8-ounce package PHILADELPHIA BRAND
   Cream Cheese, softened
1 cup PARKAY Margarine
1¹/₂ cups granulated sugar
1¹/₂ teaspoons vanilla
4 eggs
2¹/₄ cups sifted cake flour
1¹/₂ teaspoons baking powder
³/₄ cup chopped maraschino cherries, well-
   drained
¹/₂ cup chopped pecans

*   *   *

¹/₂ cup finely chopped pecans
1¹/₂ cups sifted powdered sugar
2 tablespoons milk

Combine cream cheese, margarine, granulated sugar and vanilla, mixing at medium speed on electric mixer until well blended. Add eggs, one at a time, mixing well after each addition. Sift together 2 cups flour and baking powder. Gradually add to cream cheese mixture; mix well. Toss remaining flour with cherries and pecans; fold into batter.

Grease 10-inch tube or fluted tube pan; sprinkle with finely chopped pecans. Pour batter into pan. Bake at 325°, 1 hour and 10 minutes. Cool 5 minutes; remove from pan. Cool. Glaze with combined powdered sugar and milk. Garnish with additional pecan halves and maraschino cherry halves, if desired.

10 to 12 servings

VARIATIONS
■ Substitute ³/₄ cup chopped dried apricots for maraschino cherries and 2 tablespoons orange juice and 1 teaspoon grated orange peel for milk.
■ Substitute 2 cups all-purpose flour for sifted cake flour.
■ Omit finely chopped nuts. Pour batter into three greased and floured 1-pound coffee cans. Bake at 325°, 1 hour.

MAKE AHEAD
Bake cake; wrap securely in plastic wrap. Freeze. Thaw, wrapped, at room temperature for 12 hours.

◄ *Cherry Nut Cake*

APPLE RAISIN SNACK BARS

1½ cups old fashioned or quick oats, uncooked
¾ cup flour
½ cup packed brown sugar
¼ cup granulated sugar
¾ cup PARKAY Margarine

*   *   *

2 8-ounce packages PHILADELPHIA BRAND
   Cream Cheese, softened
2 eggs
1 cup chopped apple
⅓ cup raisins
1 tablespoon granulated sugar
½ teaspoon cinnamon

Combine oats, flour and sugars; cut in margarine until mixture resembles coarse crumbs. Reserve 1 cup oat mixture; press remaining mixture onto bottom of greased 13 × 9-inch baking pan. Bake at 350°, 15 minutes.

Combine cream cheese and eggs, mixing until well blended. Pour over crust. Top with combined remaining ingredients; sprinkle with reserved oat mixture. Bake at 350°, 25 minutes. Cool; cut into bars.

Approximately 1½ dozen

VARIATION
■ Substitute *Light* PHILADELPHIA BRAND Neufchâtel Cheese for Cream Cheese.

CHILLY STRAWBERRY SOUFFLES

1 10-ounce package frozen strawberries,
   thawed
2 envelopes unflavored gelatin
2¼ cups cold water
1 8-ounce package *Light* PHILADELPHIA
   BRAND Neufchâtel Cheese, softened
¼ cup sugar
1 tablespoon lemon juice
   Few drops red food coloring (optional)
2 cups thawed frozen whipped topping

(continued)

Drain strawberries, reserving liquid. Chop strawberries. Soften gelatin in 1/2 cup water; stir over low heat until dissolved. Add remaining water. Combine neufchâtel cheese and sugar, mixing until well blended. Gradually add gelatin mixture to neufchâtel cheese mixture, mixing until well blended. Stir in reserved liquid, juice and food coloring. Chill, stirring occasionally, until thickened but not set. Beat with electric mixer or wire whisk until smooth. Fold in strawberries and whipped topping. Wrap 3-inch collar of foil around individual dessert dishes or cups; secure with tape. Pour mixture into dishes; chill until firm. Remove collar before serving.

8 to 10 servings

VARIATIONS
■ Substitute 1-quart souffle dish for individual dessert dishes.
■ Substitute PHILADELPHIA BRAND Cream Cheese for Neufchâtel Cheese. Increase sugar to 2/3 cup. Substitute 1 cup whipping cream, whipped, for whipped topping.

DELIGHTFUL DESSERT PANCAKE

1 8-ounce package *Light* PHILADELPHIA BRAND Neufchâtel Cheese, softened
3 tablespoons honey
1 teaspoon grated lemon peel
1 teaspoon lemon juice

*   *   *

1/2 cup milk
1/2 cup flour
1/4 teaspoon salt
2 eggs, beaten
1 tablespoon PARKAY Margarine
2 cups assorted fruit
1/4 cup toasted flaked coconut

Combine neufchâtel cheese, honey, peel and juice, mixing until well blended. Chill.

Gradually add milk to combined flour and salt; beat until smooth. Beat in eggs. Heat heavy 10-inch ovenproof skillet in 450° oven until very hot. Add margarine to coat skillet; pour in batter immediately. Bake on lowest oven rack at 450°, 10 minutes. Reduce oven temperature to 350°; continue baking 10 minutes or until golden brown. Fill with fruit; sprinkle with coconut. Serve immediately with neufchâtel cheese mixture.

6 to 8 servings

FAVORITE CHEESECAKE SQUARES

    1/3 cup PARKAY Margarine
    1/3 cup packed brown sugar
      1 cup flour
    1/2 cup chopped walnuts

                *   *   *

      1 8-ounce package PHILADELPHIA BRAND
        Cream Cheese, softened
    1/4 cup granulated sugar
      1 teaspoon vanilla
      1 egg
    3/4 cup multicolored milk chocolate candies

Beat margarine and brown sugar until light and fluffy. Add flour and walnuts; mix well. Reserve 1/2 cup crumb mixture; press remaining crumb mixture onto bottom of 8-inch square pan. Bake at 350°, 10 minutes.

Combine cream cheese, granulated sugar and vanilla, mixing at medium speed on electric mixer until well blended. Add egg; mix well. Layer 1/2 cup candy over crust; top with cream cheese mixture. Combine remaining candy, chopped, and reserved crumb mixture; mix well. Sprinkle crumb mixture over cream cheese mixture. Bake at 350°, 20 minutes. Cool.

16 servings

COCONUT TORTE

      1 8-ounce container Soft PHILADELPHIA
        BRAND Cream Cheese
    1/4 cup sugar
      1 tablespoon orange juice
    1/2 cup flaked coconut, toasted
    1/4 cup sliced almonds, toasted
      1 10 3/4-ounce frozen pound cake, thawed

Combine cream cheese, sugar and juice, mixing until well blended. Add coconut and almonds; mix well. Split cake into three layers. Spread layers with frosting; stack. Chill.

6 servings

Favorite Cheesecake Squares ▶

Easy "Philly" Fruit Cups

EASY "PHILLY" FRUIT CUPS

1 8-ounce package PHILADELPHIA BRAND
    Cream Cheese, softened

2 cups milk

1 3½-ounce package vanilla instant pudding
    and pie filling mix

2½ cups cubed pound cake

1½ cups strawberry slices

1 16-ounce can peach slices, drained,
    chopped

Combine cream cheese and ½ cup milk, mixing at medium speed on electric mixer until well blended. Gradually add pudding mix alternately with remaining milk; beat at low speed 1 to 2 minutes or until well blended. Place cake and fruit in individual dessert dishes. Top with pudding mixture. Garnish with frozen whipped topping, thawed, and additional fruit and fresh mint, if desired.

8 servings

VARIATIONS
■ Substitute 1½ cups fresh peach slices for canned peaches.
■ Substitute 17-ounce can apricot halves for peach slices.

BOSTON CREAM CHEESE PIE

    1 9-ounce package yellow cake mix

            *   *   *

    2 8-ounce packages PHILADELPHIA BRAND
        Cream Cheese, softened
 1/2 cup granulated sugar
    1 teaspoon vanilla
    2 eggs
 1/3 cup sour cream

            *   *   *

    2 1-ounce squares unsweetened chocolate
    3 tablespoons PARKAY Margarine
    1 cup powdered sugar
    2 tablespoons hot water
    1 teaspoon vanilla

Grease bottom of 9-inch springform pan. Prepare cake mix as directed on package; pour batter evenly into springform pan. Bake at 350°, 20 minutes.

Combine cream cheese, granulated sugar and vanilla, mixing at medium speed on electric mixer until well blended. Add eggs, one at a time, mixing well after each addition. Blend in sour cream; pour over cake layer. Bake at 350°, 35 minutes. Loosen cake from rim of pan; cool before removing rim of pan.

Melt chocolate and margarine over low heat, stirring until smooth. Remove from heat. Add remaining ingredients; mix well. Spread over cheesecake. Chill several hours. Garnish with strawberries, if desired.

10 to 12 servings

CHEESECAKE CLASSICS

ORANGE-BUTTERSCOTCH CHEESECAKE

1¹/₄ cups old fashioned or quick oats, uncooked
¹/₄ cup PARKAY Margarine, melted
¹/₄ cup packed brown sugar
 2 tablespoons flour

*   *   *

 3 8-ounce packages PHILADELPHIA BRAND
    Cream Cheese, softened
³/₄ cup granulated sugar
 2 teaspoons grated orange peel
 1 teaspoon vanilla
 4 eggs

*   *   *

¹/₂ cup packed brown sugar
¹/₃ cup light corn syrup
¹/₄ cup PARKAY Margarine, melted
 1 teaspoon vanilla

Combine oats, margarine, brown sugar and flour; press onto bottom of 9-inch springform pan. Bake at 350°, 15 minutes.

Combine cream cheese, granulated sugar, peel and vanilla, mixing at medium speed on electric mixer until well blended. Add eggs, one at a time, mixing well after each addition; pour over crust. Bake at 325°, 1 hour and 5 minutes. Loosen cake from rim of pan; cool before removing rim of pan. Chill.

Combine brown sugar, corn syrup and margarine in saucepan; bring to boil, stirring constantly. Remove from heat; stir in vanilla. Chill until slightly thickened. Spoon over cheesecake. Garnish with orange slice and fresh mint, if desired.

10 to 12 servings

Orange-Butterscotch Cheesecake ▶

Northwest Cheesecake Supreme

NORTHWEST CHEESECAKE SUPREME

   1 cup graham cracker crumbs
   3 tablespoons sugar
   3 tablespoons PARKAY Margarine, melted

*   *   *

   4 8-ounce packages PHILADELPHIA BRAND
       Cream Cheese, softened
   1 cup sugar
   3 tablespoons flour
   4 eggs
   1 cup sour cream
   1 tablespoon vanilla
   1 21-ounce can cherry pie filling

(continued)

Combine crumbs, sugar and margarine; press onto bottom of 9-inch spring-form pan. Bake at 325°, 10 minutes.

Combine cream cheese, sugar and flour, mixing at medium speed on electric mixer until well blended. Add eggs, one at a time, mixing well after each addition. Blend in sour cream and vanilla; pour over crust. Bake at 450°, 10 minutes. Reduce oven temperature to 250°; continue baking 1 hour. Loosen cake from rim of pan; cool before removing rim of pan. Chill. Top with pie filling just before serving.

10 to 12 servings

VARIATION
■ Substitute 1½ cups finely chopped nuts and 2 tablespoons sugar for graham cracker crumbs and sugar.

BANANA NUT CHEESECAKE

> 1 cup chocolate wafer crumbs
> ¼ cup PARKAY Margarine, melted
>
> *   *   *
>
> 2 8-ounce packages PHILADELPHIA BRAND
>   Cream Cheese, softened
> ½ cup sugar
> ½ cup mashed ripe banana
> 2 eggs
> ¼ cup chopped walnuts
>
> *   *   *
>
> ⅓ cup milk chocolate pieces
> 1 tablespoon PARKAY Margarine
> 2 teaspoons water

Combine crumbs and margarine; press onto bottom of 9-inch springform pan. Bake at 350°, 10 minutes.

Combine cream cheese, sugar and banana, mixing at medium speed on electric mixer until well blended. Add eggs, one at a time, mixing well after each addition. Stir in walnuts; pour over crust. Bake at 350°, 40 minutes. Loosen cake from rim of pan; cool before removing rim of pan.

Melt chocolate pieces and margarine with water over low heat, stirring until smooth. Drizzle over cheesecake. Chill.

10 to 12 servings

CARROT 'N RAISIN CHEESECAKE

1 cup graham cracker crumbs
3 tablespoons granulated sugar
1/2 teaspoon cinnamon
3 tablespoons PARKAY Margarine, melted

*   *   *

3 8-ounce packages PHILADELPHIA BRAND
    Cream Cheese, softened
1/2 cup granulated sugar
1/2 cup flour
4 eggs
1/4 cup 100% Pure KRAFT Unsweetened
    Orange Juice
1 cup finely shredded carrot
1/4 cup raisins
1/2 teaspoon ground nutmeg
1/4 teaspoon ground ginger

*   *   *

1 tablespoon 100% Pure KRAFT
    Unsweetened Orange Juice
1 cup sifted powdered sugar

Combine crumbs, granulated sugar, cinnamon and margarine; press onto bottom of 9-inch springform pan. Bake at 325°, 10 minutes.

Combine 2½ packages cream cheese, granulated sugar and ¼ cup flour, mixing at medium speed on electric mixer until well blended. Blend in eggs and juice. Add combined remaining flour, carrots, raisins and spices; mix well. Pour over crust. Bake at 450°, 10 minutes. Reduce oven temperature to 250°; continue baking 55 minutes. Loosen cake from rim of pan; cool before removing rim of pan. Chill.

Combine remaining cream cheese and juice, mixing until well blended. Gradually add powdered sugar, mixing until well blended. Spread over top of cheesecake. Garnish with additional raisins and finely shredded carrot, if desired.

10 to 12 servings

◄ *Carrot 'n Raisin Cheesecake*

CHOCOLATE RASPBERRY CHEESECAKE

1½ cups (18) finely crushed creme-filled
    chocolate cookies

2 tablespoons PARKAY Margarine, melted

*   *   *

4 8-ounce packages PHILADELPHIA BRAND
    Cream Cheese, softened

1¼ cups sugar

3 eggs

1 cup sour cream

1 teaspoon vanilla

1 6-ounce package semi-sweet chocolate
    pieces, melted

⅓ cup strained KRAFT Red Raspberry
    Preserves

*   *   *

1 6-ounce package semi-sweet chocolate
    pieces

¼ cup whipping cream

Combine crumbs and margarine; press onto bottom of 9-inch springform pan.

Combine three 8-ounce packages cream cheese and sugar, mixing at medium speed on electric mixer until well blended. Add eggs, one at a time, mixing well after each addition. Blend in sour cream and vanilla; pour over crust. Combine remaining 8-ounce package cream cheese and melted chocolate, mixing at medium speed on electric mixer until well blended. Add preserves; mix well. Drop rounded measuring tablespoonfuls of chocolate cream cheese batter over plain cream cheese batter; do not swirl. Bake at 325°, 1 hour and 20 minutes. Loosen cake from rim of pan; cool before removing rim of pan.

Melt chocolate pieces and whipping cream over low heat, stirring until smooth. Spread over cheesecake. Chill. Garnish with additional whipping cream, whipped, raspberries and fresh mint leaves, if desired.

10 to 12 servings

SUN-SATIONAL CHEESECAKE

      1 cup graham cracker crumbs
      3 tablespoons sugar
      3 tablespoons PARKAY Margarine, melted
                *   *   *
      3 8-ounce packages PHILADELPHIA BRAND
          Cream Cheese, softened
      1 cup sugar
      3 tablespoons flour
      2 tablespoons lemon juice
      1 tablespoon grated lemon peel
    ¹/₂ teaspoon vanilla
      4 eggs (1 separated)
                *   *   *
    ³/₄ cup sugar
      2 tablespoons cornstarch
    ¹/₂ cup water
    ¹/₄ cup lemon juice

Combine crumbs, sugar and margarine; press onto bottom of 9-inch spring-form pan. Bake at 325°, 10 minutes.

Combine cream cheese, sugar, flour, juice, peel and vanilla, mixing at medium speed on electric mixer until well blended. Add three eggs, one at a time, mixing well after each addition. Beat in remaining egg white; reserve yolk for glaze. Pour over crust. Bake at 450°, 10 minutes. Reduce oven temperature to 250°; continue baking 30 minutes. Loosen cake from rim of pan; cool before removing rim of pan.

Combine sugar and cornstarch in saucepan; stir in water and juice. Cook, stirring constantly, until clear and thickened. Add small amount of hot mixture to slightly beaten egg yolk. Return to hot mixture; cook 3 minutes, stirring constantly. Cool slightly. Spoon over cheesecake; chill.

10 to 12 servings

VERY BLUEBERRY CHEESECAKE

1¹/₂ cups vanilla wafer crumbs
¹/₄ cup PARKAY Margarine, melted

* * *

1 envelope unflavored gelatin
¹/₄ cup cold water
2 8-ounce packages PHILADELPHIA BRAND
    Cream Cheese, softened
1 tablespoon lemon juice
1 teaspoon grated lemon peel
1 7-ounce jar KRAFT Marshmallow Creme
1 8-ounce container (3 cups) frozen whipped
    topping, thawed
2 cups blueberries

Combine crumbs and margarine; press onto bottom of 9-inch springform pan. Chill.

Soften gelatin in water; stir over low heat until dissolved. Gradually add gelatin to cream cheese, mixing at medium speed on electric mixer until well blended. Blend in juice and peel. Beat in marshmallow creme; fold in whipped topping. Puree blueberries; fold into cream cheese mixture. Pour over crust. Chill until firm. Garnish with additional frozen whipped topping, thawed, and lemon peel, if desired.

10 to 12 servings

VARIATIONS
■ Substitute *Light* PHILADELPHIA BRAND Neufchâtel
Cheese for Cream Cheese.
■ Substitute strawberry slices for blueberries.
■ Substitute raspberries for blueberries.

◄ *Very Blueberry Cheesecake*

COCOA-NUT MERINGUE CHEESECAKE

1 7-ounce package flaked coconut, toasted
¼ cup chopped pecans
3 tablespoons PARKAY Margarine, melted

*   *   *

2 8-ounce packages PHILADELPHIA BRAND
    Cream Cheese, softened
⅓ cup sugar
3 tablespoons cocoa
2 tablespoons water
1 teaspoon vanilla
3 eggs, separated

*   *   *

Dash of salt
1 7-ounce jar KRAFT Marshmallow Creme
½ cup chopped pecans

Combine coconut, pecans and margarine; press onto bottom of 9-inch spring-form pan.

Combine cream cheese, sugar, cocoa, water and vanilla, mixing at medium speed on electric mixer until well blended. Blend in egg yolks; pour over crust. Bake at 350°, 30 minutes. Loosen cake from rim of pan; cool before removing rim of pan.

Beat egg whites and salt until foamy; gradually add marshmallow creme, beating until stiff peaks form. Sprinkle pecans over cheesecake to within ½-inch of outer edge. Carefully spread marshmallow creme mixture over top of cheesecake to seal. Bake at 350°, 15 minutes. Cool.

10 to 12 servings

◄ *Cocoa-Nut Meringue Cheesecake*

Festive Irish Cream Cheesecake

FESTIVE IRISH CREAM CHEESECAKE

1 cup graham cracker crumbs

¼ cup sugar

¼ cup PARKAY Margarine, melted

*   *   *

1 envelope unflavored gelatin

½ cup cold water

1 cup sugar

3 eggs, separated

2 8-ounce packages PHILADELPHIA BRAND
   Cream Cheese, softened

2 tablespoons cocoa

2 tablespoons bourbon

1 cup whipping cream, whipped

(continued)

160

Combine crumbs, sugar and margarine; press onto bottom of 9-inch spring-form pan.

Soften gelatin in water; stir over low heat until dissolved. Blend in ¾ cup sugar and beaten egg yolks; cook, stirring constantly, over low heat 3 minutes. Combine cream cheese and cocoa, mixing at medium speed on electric mixer until well blended. Gradually add gelatin mixture and bourbon, mixing until blended. Chill until thickened but not set. Beat egg whites until foamy; gradually add remaining sugar, beating until stiff peaks form. Fold egg whites and whipped cream into cream cheese mixture; pour over crust. Chill until firm. Garnish with chocolate curls and small silver candy balls, if desired.

10 to 12 servings

VARIATION
■ Substitute 2 tablespoons cold coffee for bourbon.

COOKIES AND CREAM CHEESECAKE

2 cups (24) crushed creme-filled chocolate
    cookies
6 tablespoons PARKAY Margarine, softened

*   *   *

1 envelope unflavored gelatin
¼ cup cold water
1 8-ounce package PHILADELPHIA BRAND
    Cream Cheese, softened
½ cup sugar
¾ cup milk
1 cup whipping cream, whipped
1¼ cups (10) coarsely chopped creme-filled
    chocolate cookies

Combine cookie crumbs and margarine; press onto bottom and sides of 9-inch springform pan.

Soften gelatin in water; stir over low heat until dissolved. Combine cream cheese and sugar, mixing at medium speed on electric mixer until well blended. Gradually add gelatin and milk, mixing until blended. Chill until mixture is thickened but not set. Fold in whipped cream. Reserve 1½ cups cream cheese mixture; pour remaining cream cheese mixture over crust. Top with cookies and reserved cream cheese mixture. Chill until firm.

8 servings

VERY SMOOTH CHEESECAKE

1 cup graham cracker crumbs
3 tablespoons sugar
3 tablespoons PARKAY Margarine, melted

*   *   *

1 envelope unflavored gelatin
1/4 cup cold water
1 8-ounce package PHILADELPHIA BRAND
    Cream Cheese, softened
1/2 cup sugar
1 10-ounce package frozen strawberries,
    thawed
   Milk
1 cup whipping cream, whipped

Combine crumbs, sugar and margarine; press onto bottom of 9-inch spring-form pan. Bake at 325°, 10 minutes. Cool.

Soften gelatin in water; stir over low heat until dissolved. Combine cream cheese and sugar, mixing at medium speed on electric mixer until well blended. Drain strawberries, reserving liquid. Add enough milk to liquid to measure 1 cup. Gradually add combined milk mixture and gelatin to cream cheese, mixing until blended. Chill until slightly thickened. Fold in whipped cream and strawberries; pour over crust. Chill until firm.

10 to 12 servings

VARIATION
■ Substitute 1 cup vanilla wafer crumbs, 1/2 cup chopped nuts, 2 tablespoons sugar and 2 tablespoons margarine for graham cracker crumbs, sugar and margarine.

LATTICE CHERRY CHEESECAKE

1 20-ounce package PILLSBURY'S BEST
   Refrigerated Sugar Cookies

       *   *   *

2 8-ounce packages PHILADELPHIA BRAND
   Cream Cheese, softened

1 cup sour cream

3/4 cup sugar

1/4 teaspoon almond extract

3 eggs

1 21-ounce can cherry pie filling

Freeze cookie dough 1 hour. Slice into 1/8-inch slices. Arrange slices, slightly overlapping, on bottom and sides of greased 9-inch springform pan. With lightly floured fingers, seal edges to form crust.

Combine cream cheese, sour cream, sugar and extract, mixing at medium speed on electric mixer until well blended. Add eggs, one at a time, mixing well after each addition. Reserve 1/4 cup batter; chill. Pour remaining batter over crust. Bake at 350°, 1 hour and 10 minutes. Increase oven temperature to 450°. Spoon pie filling over cheesecake. Spoon reserved batter over pie filling in criss-cross pattern to form lattice design. Bake at 450°, 10 minutes. Loosen cake from rim of pan; cool before removing rim of pan.

10 to 12 servings

VARIATION

■ Substitute 13 × 9-inch baking pan for 9-inch springform pan. Prepare as directed except for baking. Bake at 350°, 40 minutes. Increase oven temperature to 450°. Continue as directed.

Autumn Cheesecake

1 cup graham cracker crumbs
3 tablespoons sugar
1/2 teaspoon cinnamon
1/4 cup PARKAY Margarine, melted

* * *

2 8-ounce packages PHILADELPHIA BRAND
    Cream Cheese, softened
1/2 cup sugar
2 eggs
1/2 teaspoon vanilla

* * *

4 cups thin peeled apple slices
1/3 cup sugar
1/2 teaspoon cinnamon
1/4 cup chopped pecans

Combine crumbs, sugar, cinnamon and margarine; press onto bottom of 9-inch springform pan. Bake at 350°, 10 minutes.

Combine cream cheese and sugar, mixing at medium speed on electric mixer until well blended. Add eggs, one at a time, mixing well after each addition. Blend in vanilla; pour over crust.

Toss apples with combined sugar and cinnamon. Spoon apple mixture over cream cheese layer; sprinkle with pecans. Bake at 350°, 1 hour and 10 minutes. Loosen cake from rim of pan; cool before removing rim of pan. Chill.

10 to 12 servings

VARIATION
■ Add 1/2 cup finely chopped pecans with crumbs for crust. Continue as directed.

Autumn Cheesecake ▶

CHOCOLATE VELVET CHEESECAKE

1 cup vanilla wafer crumbs

1/2 cup chopped pecans

3 tablespoons granulated sugar

1/4 cup PARKAY Margarine, melted

*   *   *

2 8-ounce packages PHILADELPHIA BRAND
  Cream Cheese, softened

1/2 cup packed brown sugar

2 eggs

1 6-ounce package semi-sweet chocolate
  pieces, melted

3 tablespoons almond flavored liqueur

*   *   *

2 cups sour cream

2 tablespoons granulated sugar

Combine crumbs, pecans, granulated sugar and margarine; press onto bottom of 9-inch springform pan. Bake at 325°, 10 minutes.

Combine cream cheese and brown sugar, mixing at medium speed on electric mixer until well blended. Add eggs, one at a time, mixing well after each addition. Blend in chocolate and liqueur; pour over crust. Bake at 325°, 35 minutes.

Increase oven temperature to 425°. Combine sour cream and granulated sugar; carefully spread over cheesecake. Bake at 425°, 10 minutes. Loosen cake from rim of pan; cool before removing rim of pan. Chill.

10 to 12 servings

VARIATION

■ Substitute 2 tablespoons milk and 1/4 teaspoon almond extract for almond flavored liqueur.

Marble Cheesecake

MARBLE CHEESECAKE

        1 cup graham cracker crumbs
        3 tablespoons sugar
        3 tablespoons PARKAY Margarine, melted

                    *   *   *

        3 8-ounce packages PHILADELPHIA BRAND
            Cream Cheese, softened
    3/4 cup sugar
        1 teaspoon vanilla
        3 eggs
        1 1-ounce square unsweetened chocolate,
            melted

Combine crumbs, sugar and margarine; press onto bottom of 9-inch spring-form pan. Bake at 350°, 10 minutes.

Combine cream cheese, sugar and vanilla, mixing at medium speed on electric mixer until well blended. Add eggs, one at a time, mixing well after each addition. Blend chocolate into 1 cup batter. Spoon plain and chocolate batters alternately over crust; cut through batters with knife several times for marble effect. Bake at 450°, 10 minutes. Reduce oven temperature to 250°; continue baking 30 minutes. Loosen cake from rim of pan; cool before removing rim of pan. Chill.

10 to 12 servings

GALA APRICOT CHEESECAKE

2¼ cups quick oats, uncooked
⅓ cup packed brown sugar
3 tablespoons flour
⅓ cup PARKAY Margarine, melted

*   *   *

1 envelope unflavored gelatin
⅓ cup cold water
2 8-ounce packages PHILADELPHIA BRAND
    Cream Cheese, softened
½ cup granulated sugar
2 tablespoons brandy
½ cup finely chopped dried apricots
1 cup whipping cream, whipped

*   *   *

1 10-ounce jar KRAFT Apricot Preserves
1 tablespoon brandy

Combine oats, brown sugar, flour and margarine; press onto bottom and 1½-inches up sides of 9-inch springform pan. Bake at 350°, 15 minutes. Cool.

Soften gelatin in water; stir over low heat until dissolved. Combine cream cheese and granulated sugar, mixing at medium speed on electric mixer until well blended. Gradually add gelatin and brandy to cream cheese mixture, mixing until well blended. Chill until slightly thickened; fold in apricots and whipped cream. Pour into crust; chill until firm.

Heat combined preserves and brandy over low heat; cool. Spoon over cheesecake.

10 to 12 servings

VARIATION
■ Substitute *Light* PHILADELPHIA BRAND Neufchâtel Cheese for Cream Cheese.

Gala Apricot Cheesecake ▶

PRALINE CHEESECAKE

1 cup graham cracker crumbs
3 tablespoons granulated sugar
3 tablespoons PARKAY Margarine, melted

*   *   *

3 8-ounce packages PHILADELPHIA BRAND
   Cream Cheese, softened
3/4 cup packed dark brown sugar
2 tablespoons flour
3 eggs
2 teaspoons vanilla
1/2 cup finely chopped pecans
   Maple syrup
   Pecan halves

Combine crumbs, granulated sugar and margarine; press onto bottom of 9-inch springform pan. Bake at 350°, 10 minutes.

Combine cream cheese, brown sugar and flour, mixing at medium speed on electric mixer until well blended. Add eggs, one at a time, mixing well after each addition. Blend in vanilla; stir in chopped pecans. Pour over crust. Bake at 450°, 10 minutes. Reduce oven temperature to 250°; continue baking 30 minutes. Loosen cake from rim of pan; cool before removing rim of pan. Chill. Brush with syrup; top with pecan halves.

10 to 12 servings

HEAVENLY DESSERT CHEESECAKE

1 tablespoon graham cracker crumbs
1 cup low fat (1% to 2%) cottage cheese
2 8-ounce packages *Light* PHILADELPHIA
   BRAND Neufchâtel Cheese, softened
2/3 cup sugar
2 tablespoons flour
3 eggs
2 tablespoons skim milk
1/4 teaspoon almond extract

(continued)

Lightly grease bottom of 9-inch springform pan. Sprinkle with crumbs. Dust bottom; remove excess crumbs. Place cottage cheese in blender container. Cover; process on high speed until smooth. In large mixing bowl of electric mixer, combine cottage cheese, neufchâtel cheese, sugar and flour, mixing at medium speed until well blended. Add eggs, one at a time, mixing well after each addition. Blend in milk and extract; pour into pan. Bake at 325°, 45 to 50 minutes or until center is almost set. (Center of cheesecake appears soft but firms upon cooling.) Loosen cake from rim of pan; cool before removing rim of pan. Chill. Top with fresh strawberry slices or blueberries, if desired.

10 to 12 servings

VARIATION

■ Prepare pan as directed; omit blender method. Place cottage cheese in large bowl of electric mixer; beat cottage cheese at high speed until smooth. Add neufchâtel cheese, sugar and flour, mixing at medium speed until well blended. Continue as directed.

LEMON DELIGHT CHEESECAKE

1½ cups graham cracker crumbs
¼ cup sugar
½ cup PARKAY Margarine, melted

* * *

1 envelope unflavored gelatin
⅓ cup cold water
⅓ cup lemon juice
3 eggs, separated
½ cup sugar
1 teaspoon grated lemon peel
2 8-ounce containers Soft PHILADELPHIA
　BRAND Cream Cheese

Combine crumbs, sugar and margarine; reserve ½ cup. Press remaining crumb mixture onto bottom of 9-inch springform pan.

Soften gelatin in water; stir over low heat until dissolved. Add juice, egg yolks, ¼ cup sugar and peel; cook, stirring constantly, over medium heat 5 minutes. Gradually add to cream cheese, mixing at medium speed on electric mixer until well blended. Beat egg whites until foamy; gradually add remaining sugar, beating until stiff peaks form. Fold into cream cheese mixture; pour over crust. Top with reserved crumbs; chill until firm.

10 to 12 servings

TEMPTING TRIFLE CHEESECAKE

1½ cups soft coconut macaroon cookie crumbs

*   *   *

3 8-ounce packages PHILADELPHIA BRAND
Cream Cheese, softened

¾ cup sugar

4 eggs

½ cup sour cream

½ cup whipping cream

2 tablespoons sweet sherry

1 teaspoon vanilla

*   *   *

1 10-ounce jar KRAFT Red Raspberry
Preserves

½ cup whipping cream, whipped

Toasted slivered almonds

Press crumbs onto bottom of greased 9-inch springform pan. Bake at 325°, 15 minutes.

Combine cream cheese and sugar, mixing at medium speed on electric mixer until well blended. Add eggs, one at a time, mixing well after each addition. Blend in sour cream, whipping cream, sherry and vanilla; pour over crust. Bake at 325°, 1 hour and 10 minutes. Loosen cake from rim of pan; cool before removing rim of pan. Chill.

Heat preserves in saucepan over low heat until melted. Strain to remove seeds. Spoon over cheesecake, spreading to edges. Dollop with whipped cream; top with almonds.

10 to 12 servings

Creamy Chilled Cheesecake

CREAMY CHILLED CHEESECAKE

1 cup graham cracker crumbs

$1/4$ cup sugar

$1/4$ cup PARKAY Margarine, melted

*   *   *

1 envelope unflavored gelatin

$1/4$ cup cold water

1 8-ounce package PHILADELPHIA BRAND
  Cream Cheese, softened

$1/2$ cup sugar

$3/4$ cup milk

$1/4$ cup lemon juice

1 cup whipping cream, whipped

Strawberry halves

Combine crumbs, sugar and margarine; press onto bottom of 9-inch spring-form pan.

Soften gelatin in water; stir over low heat until dissolved. Combine cream cheese and sugar, mixing at medium speed on electric mixer until well blended. Gradually add gelatin, milk and juice, mixing until blended. Chill until slightly thickened; fold in whipped cream. Pour over crust; chill until firm. Top with strawberries just before serving.

8 servings

RUM RAISIN CHEESECAKE

    1 cup old fashioned or quick oats, uncooked
  ¼ cup chopped nuts
    3 tablespoons packed brown sugar
    3 tablespoons PARKAY Margarine, melted

                    *   *   *

    2 8-ounce packages PHILADELPHIA BRAND
        Cream Cheese, softened
  ⅓ cup granulated sugar
  ¼ cup flour
    2 eggs
  ½ cup sour cream
    3 tablespoons rum
    2 tablespoons PARKAY Margarine
  ⅓ cup packed brown sugar
  ⅓ cup raisins
  ¼ cup chopped nuts
    2 tablespoons old fashioned or quick oats,
        uncooked

Combine oats, nuts, brown sugar and margarine; press onto bottom of 9-inch springform pan. Bake at 350°, 15 minutes.

Combine cream cheese, granulated sugar and 2 tablespoons flour, mixing at medium speed on electric mixer until well blended. Add eggs, one at a time, mixing well after each addition. Blend in sour cream and rum; mix well. Pour over crust. Cut margarine into combined remaining flour and brown sugar until mixture resembles coarse crumbs. Stir in raisins, nuts and oats. Sprinkle over cream cheese mixture. Bake at 350°, 50 minutes. Loosen cake from rim of pan; cool before removing rim of pan.

10 to 12 servings

Top: Rum Raisin Cheesecake
◄*Bottom: Aloha Cheesecake (see page 176)*

ALOHA CHEESECAKE

1 cup vanilla wafer crumbs
1/4 cup PARKAY Margarine, melted

* * *

2 8-ounce packages PHILADELPHIA BRAND
  Cream Cheese, softened
1/3 cup sugar
2 tablespoons milk
2 eggs
1/2 cup chopped macadamia nuts, toasted
1 8 1/4-ounce can crushed pineapple, drained
1 kiwi, peeled, sliced

Combine crumbs and margarine; press onto bottom of 9-inch springform pan. Bake at 350°, 10 minutes.

Combine cream cheese, sugar and milk, mixing at medium speed on electric mixer until well blended. Add eggs, one at a time, mixing well after each addition. Stir in nuts; pour over crust. Bake at 350°, 45 minutes. Loosen cake from rim of pan; cool before removing rim of pan. Chill. Before serving, top with fruit.

10 to 12 servings

CHOCOLATE CHIP CHEESECAKE SUPREME

1 cup chocolate wafer crumbs
3 tablespoons PARKAY Margarine, melted

* * *

3 8-ounce packages PHILADELPHIA BRAND
  Cream Cheese, softened
3/4 cup sugar
1/4 cup flour
3 eggs
1/2 cup sour cream
1 teaspoon vanilla
1 cup mini semi-sweet chocolate pieces

(continued)

Combine crumbs and margarine; press onto bottom of 9-inch springform pan. Bake at 350°, 10 minutes.

Combine cream cheese, sugar and flour, mixing at medium speed on electric mixer until well blended. Add eggs, one at a time, mixing well after each addition. Blend in sour cream and vanilla. Stir in chocolate pieces; pour over crust. Bake at 325°, 55 minutes. Loosen cake from rim of pan; cool before removing rim of pan. Chill. Garnish with whipped cream and fresh mint, if desired.

10 to 12 servings

Chocolate Chip Cheesecake Supreme

ROCKY ROAD CHEESECAKE

1 cup chocolate wafer crumbs
3 tablespoons PARKAY Margarine, melted

       *   *   *

1 envelope unflavored gelatin
1/4 cup cold water
2 8-ounce containers Soft PHILADELPHIA
    BRAND Cream Cheese
3/4 cup sugar
1/3 cup cocoa
1/2 teaspoon vanilla
2 cups KRAFT Miniature Marshmallows
1 cup whipping cream, whipped
1/2 cup chopped nuts

Combine crumbs and margarine; press onto bottom of 9-inch springform pan. Bake at 350°, 10 minutes. Cool.

Soften gelatin in water; stir over low heat until dissolved. Combine cream cheese, sugar, cocoa and vanilla, mixing at medium speed on electric mixer until well blended. Gradually add gelatin, mixing until blended. Fold in remaining ingredients; pour over crust. Chill until firm.   *10 to 12 servings*

CAPPUCCINO CHEESECAKE

1 1/2 cups finely chopped nuts
2 tablespoons sugar
3 tablespoons PARKAY Margarine, melted

       *   *   *

4 8-ounce packages PHILADELPHIA BRAND
    Cream Cheese, softened
1 cup sugar
3 tablespoons flour
4 eggs
1 cup sour cream
1 tablespoon instant coffee granules
1/4 teaspoon cinnamon
1/4 cup boiling water

(continued)

Combine nuts, sugar and margarine; press onto bottom of 9-inch springform pan. Bake at 325°, 10 minutes.

Combine cream cheese, sugar and flour, mixing at medium speed on electric mixer until well blended. Add eggs, one at a time, mixing well after each addition. Blend in sour cream. Dissolve coffee granules and cinnamon in water. Cool; gradually add to cream cheese mixture, mixing until well blended. Pour over crust. Bake at 450°, 10 minutes. Reduce oven temperature to 250°; continue baking 1 hour. Loosen cake from rim of pan; cool before removing rim of pan. Chill. Garnish with whipped cream and whole coffee beans, if desired.

10 to 12 servings

LIME DELICIOUS CHEESECAKE

  1¼ **cups zwieback toast crumbs**
    2 **tablespoons sugar**
  ⅓ **cup PARKAY Margarine, melted**

        *   *   *

    1 **envelope unflavored gelatin**
  ¼ **cup cold water**
  ¼ **cup lime juice**
    3 **eggs, separated**
  ½ **cup sugar**
  1½ **teaspoons grated lime peel**
    2 **8-ounce packages** *Light* **PHILADELPHIA BRAND Neufchâtel Cheese, softened**
      Few drops green food coloring (optional)
    2 **cups thawed frozen whipped topping**

Combine crumbs, sugar and margarine; press onto bottom of 9-inch springform pan. Bake at 325°, 10 minutes. Cool.

Soften gelatin in water; stir over low heat until dissolved. Add juice, egg yolks, ¼ cup sugar and peel; cook, stirring constantly, over medium heat 5 minutes. Cool. Gradually add gelatin mixture to neufchâtel cheese, mixing at medium speed on electric mixer until well blended. Stir in food coloring. Beat egg whites until foamy; gradually add remaining sugar, beating until stiff peaks form. Fold egg whites and whipped topping into neufchâtel cheese mixture; pour over crust. Chill until firm. Garnish with additional lime peel, if desired.

10 to 12 servings

Amaretto Peach Cheesecake

AMARETTO PEACH CHEESECAKE

   3 tablespoons PARKAY Margarine
$1/3$ cup sugar
   1 egg
$3/4$ cup flour

*   *   *

   3 8-ounce packages PHILADELPHIA BRAND
      Cream Cheese, softened
$3/4$ cup sugar
   3 tablespoons flour
   3 eggs
   1 16-ounce can peach halves, drained, pureed
$1/4$ cup almond flavored liqueur

(continued)

Combine margarine and sugar until light and fluffy. Blend in egg. Add flour; mix well. Spread dough onto bottom of 9-inch springform pan. Bake at 450°, 10 minutes.

Combine cream cheese, sugar and flour, mixing at medium speed on electric mixer until well blended. Add eggs, one at a time, mixing well after each addition. Add peaches and liqueur; mix well. Pour over crust. Bake at 450°, 10 minutes. Reduce oven temperature to 250°; continue baking 65 minutes. Loosen cake from rim of pan; cool before removing rim of pan. Chill. Garnish with additional peach slices and sliced almonds, toasted, if desired.

10 to 12 servings

Holiday eggnog cheesecake

    1 cup graham cracker crumbs
$1/4$ cup sugar
$1/4$ teaspoon ground nutmeg
$1/4$ cup PARKAY Margarine, melted

               *   *   *

    1 envelope unflavored gelatin
$1/4$ cup cold water
    1 8-ounce package PHILADELPHIA BRAND
       Cream Cheese, softened
$1/4$ cup sugar
    1 cup eggnog
    1 cup whipping cream, whipped

Combine crumbs, sugar, nutmeg and margarine; press onto bottom of 9-inch springform pan.

Soften gelatin in water; stir over low heat until dissolved. Combine cream cheese and sugar, mixing at medium speed on electric mixer until well blended. Gradually add gelatin and eggnog, mixing until blended. Chill until slightly thickened; fold in whipped cream. Pour over crust; chill until firm.

10 to 12 servings

VARIATION
■ Increase sugar to $1/3$ cup. Substitute milk for eggnog. Add 1 teaspoon vanilla and $3/4$ teaspoon rum extract. Continue as directed.

MINIATURE CHEESECAKES

        1/3 cup graham cracker crumbs
          1 tablespoon sugar
          1 tablespoon PARKAY Margarine, melted

                    *   *   *

          1 8-ounce package PHILADELPHIA BRAND
            Cream Cheese, softened
        1/4 cup sugar
      1 1/2 teaspoons lemon juice
        1/2 teaspoon grated lemon peel
        1/4 teaspoon vanilla
          1 egg
            KRAFT Strawberry or Apricot Preserves

Combine crumbs, sugar and margarine. Press rounded measuring tablespoonful of crumb mixture onto bottom of each of six paper-lined muffin cups. Bake
at 325°, 5 minutes.

Combine cream cheese, sugar, juice, peel and vanilla, mixing at medium speed
on electric mixer until well blended. Blend in egg; pour over crust, filling each
cup 3/4 full. Bake at 325°, 25 minutes. Cool before removing from pan. Chill.
Top with preserves just before serving.

6 servings

VARIATION
■ Substitute fresh fruit for KRAFT Preserves.

MAKE AHEAD
Wrap chilled cheesecakes individually in plastic wrap; freeze.
Let stand at room temperature 40 minutes before serving.

Miniature Cheesecakes ▶

PEPPERMINT CHEESECAKE

1 cup chocolate wafer crumbs
3 tablespoons PARKAY Margarine, melted

*   *   *

1 envelope unflavored gelatin
1/4 cup cold water
2 8-ounce containers Soft PHILADELPHIA
    BRAND Cream Cheese
1/2 cup sugar
1/2 cup milk
1/4 cup crushed peppermint candy
1 cup whipping cream, whipped
2 1.45-ounce milk chocolate candy bars,
    finely chopped

Combine crumbs and margarine; press onto bottom of 9-inch springform pan. Bake at 350°, 10 minutes. Cool.

Soften gelatin in water; stir over low heat until dissolved. Combine cream cheese and sugar, mixing at medium speed on electric mixer until well blended. Gradually add gelatin, milk and peppermint candy, mixing until blended; chill until thickened but not set. Fold in whipped cream and chocolate; pour over crust. Chill until firm. Garnish with additional whipping cream, whipped, combined with crushed peppermint candy, if desired.

10 to 12 servings

Peppermint Cheesecake ▶

CHOCOLATE MINT MERINGUE CHEESECAKE

1 cup chocolate wafer crumbs
3 tablespoons PARKAY Margarine, melted
2 tablespoons sugar

*　　*　　*

3 8-ounce packages PHILADELPHIA BRAND
   Cream Cheese, softened
2/3 cup sugar
3 eggs
1 cup mint chocolate pieces, melted
1 teaspoon vanilla

*　　*　　*

3 egg whites
1 7-ounce jar KRAFT Marshmallow Creme

Combine crumbs, margarine and sugar; press onto bottom of 9-inch spring-form pan. Bake at 350°, 10 minutes.

Combine cream cheese and sugar, mixing at medium speed on electric mixer until well blended. Add eggs, one at a time, mixing well after each addition. Blend in mint chocolate and vanilla; pour over crust. Bake at 350°, 50 minutes. Loosen cake from rim of pan; cool before removing rim of pan. Chill.

Beat egg whites until soft peaks form. Gradually add marshmallow creme, beating until stiff peaks form. Carefully spread over top of cheesecake to seal. Bake at 450°, 3 to 4 minutes or until lightly browned.

10 to 12 servings

VARIATION
■ Substitute *Light* PHILADELPHIA BRAND Neufchâtel Cheese for Cream Cheese.

"PHILLY" CHEESECAKE

²/₃ cup graham cracker crumbs

2 tablespoons PARKAY Margarine, melted

*   *   *

2 8-ounce packages PHILADELPHIA BRAND
    Cream Cheese, softened

¹/₂ cup sugar

1 tablespoon lemon juice

1 teaspoon grated lemon peel

¹/₂ teaspoon vanilla

2 eggs, separated

Combine crumbs and margarine; press onto bottom of 7-inch springform pan. Bake at 325°, 10 minutes.

Combine cream cheese, sugar, juice, peel and vanilla, mixing at medium speed on electric mixer until well blended. Add egg yolks, one at a time, mixing well after each addition. Beat egg whites until stiff peaks form; fold into cream cheese mixture. Pour over crust. Bake at 300°, 55 minutes. Loosen cake from rim of pan; cool before removing rim of pan. Chill. Top with cherry pie filling or fresh fruit, if desired.

8 servings

VARIATION

■ For 9-inch cheesecake:

1 cup graham cracker crumbs

3 tablespoons PARKAY Margarine, melted

*   *   *

3 8-ounce packages PHILADELPHIA BRAND
    Cream Cheese, softened

³/₄ cup sugar

5 teaspoons lemon juice

1¹/₂ teaspoons grated lemon peel

1 teaspoon vanilla

3 eggs, separated

Combine crumbs and margarine; press onto bottom of 9-inch springform pan. Bake as directed.

Prepare filling as directed. Pour over crust. Bake at 300°, 45 minutes. Continue as directed.

10 to 12 servings

CHERRY CHEESECAKE

1 cup graham cracker crumbs

3 tablespoons sugar

3 tablespoons PARKAY Margarine, melted

*   *   *

3 8-ounce packages PHILADELPHIA BRAND
   Cream Cheese, softened

3/4 cup sugar

3 eggs

1 teaspoon vanilla

1 21-ounce can cherry pie filling

Combine crumbs, sugar and margarine; press onto bottom of 9-inch spring-form pan. Bake at 325°, 10 minutes.

Combine cream cheese and sugar, mixing at medium speed on electric mixer until well blended. Add eggs, one at a time, mixing well after each addition. Blend in vanilla; pour over crust. Bake at 450°, 10 minutes. Reduce oven temperature to 250°; continue baking 25 to 30 minutes or until set. Loosen cake from rim of pan; cool before removing rim of pan. Chill. Top with pie filling just before serving.

10 to 12 servings

PUMPKIN MARBLE CHEESECAKE

1 1/2 cups gingersnap crumbs

1/2 cup finely chopped pecans

1/3 cup PARKAY Margarine, melted

*   *   *

2 8-ounce packages PHILADELPHIA BRAND
   Cream Cheese, softened

3/4 cup sugar

1 teaspoon vanilla

3 eggs

1 cup canned pumpkin

3/4 teaspoon cinnamon

1/4 teaspoon ground nutmeg

(continued)

Combine crumbs, pecans and margarine; press onto bottom and 1½-inches up sides of 9-inch springform pan. Bake at 350°, 10 minutes.

Combine cream cheese, ½ cup sugar and vanilla, mixing at medium speed on electric mixer until well blended. Add eggs, one at a time, mixing well after each addition. Reserve 1 cup batter. Add remaining sugar, pumpkin and spices to remaining batter; mix well. Alternately layer pumpkin and cream cheese batters over crust. Cut through batters with knife several times for marble effect. Bake at 350°, 55 minutes. Loosen cake from rim of pan; cool before removing rim of pan. Chill.

10 to 12 servings

Pumpkin Marble Cheesecake

BLACK FOREST CHEESECAKE DELIGHT

1 cup chocolate wafer crumbs
3 tablespoons PARKAY Margarine, melted

*   *   *

2 8-ounce packages PHILADELPHIA BRAND
    Cream Cheese, softened
2/3 cup sugar
2 eggs
1 6-ounce package semi-sweet chocolate
    pieces, melted
1/4 teaspoon almond extract

*   *   *

1 21-ounce can cherry pie filling
    Frozen whipped topping, thawed

Combine crumbs and margarine; press onto bottom of 9-inch springform pan. Bake at 350°, 10 minutes.

Combine cream cheese and sugar, mixing at medium speed on electric mixer until well blended. Add eggs, one at a time, mixing well after each addition. Blend in chocolate and extract; pour over crust. Bake at 350°, 45 minutes. Loosen cake from rim of pan; cool before removing rim of pan. Chill.

Top cheesecake with pie filling and whipped topping just before serving.

10 to 12 servings

◄ *Black Forest Cheesecake Delight*

ORANGE UPSIDE-DOWN CHEESECAKE

1 envelope unflavored gelatin
1½ cups KRAFT 100% Pure Unsweetened
    Orange Juice
¼ cup sugar
2 cups orange sections

*   *   *

1 envelope unflavored gelatin
½ cup KRAFT 100% Pure Unsweetened
    Orange Juice
3 8-ounce packages PHILADELPHIA BRAND
    Cream Cheese, softened
1 cup sugar
2 teaspoons grated orange peel
1 cup whipping cream, whipped

*   *   *

1 cup vanilla wafer crumbs
½ teaspoon cinnamon
3 tablespoons PARKAY Margarine, melted

Soften gelatin in juice. Add sugar; stir over low heat until dissolved. Chill until slightly thickened. Arrange orange sections on bottom of 9-inch springform pan. Pour gelatin mixture over oranges; chill until thickened but not set.

Soften gelatin in juice; stir over low heat until dissolved. Combine cream cheese, sugar and peel, mixing at medium speed on electric mixer until well blended. Gradually add gelatin mixture, mixing until blended. Chill until slightly thickened; fold in whipped cream. Pour over oranges; chill.

Combine crumbs, cinnamon and margarine; gently press onto top of cake. Chill. Loosen cake from rim of pan; invert onto serving plate. Remove rim of pan.

10 to 12 servings

VARIATION
■ Omit cinnamon. Substitute graham cracker crumbs or chocolate wafer crumbs for vanilla wafer crumbs.

Chocolate Turtle Cheesecake

CHOCOLATE TURTLE CHEESECAKE

2 cups vanilla wafer crumbs
6 tablespoons PARKAY Margarine, melted

*   *   *

1 14-ounce bag KRAFT Caramels
1 5-ounce can evaporated milk
1 cup chopped pecans, toasted
2 8-ounce packages PHILADELPHIA BRAND
    Cream Cheese, softened
1/2 cup sugar
1 teaspoon vanilla
2 eggs
1/2 cup semi-sweet chocolate pieces, melted

Combine crumbs and margarine; press onto bottom and sides of 9-inch spring-form pan. Bake at 350°, 10 minutes.

In 1½-quart heavy saucepan, melt caramels with milk over low heat, stirring frequently, until smooth. Pour over crust. Top with pecans. Combine cream cheese, sugar and vanilla, mixing at medium speed on electric mixer until well blended. Add eggs, one at a time, mixing well after each addition. Blend in chocolate; pour over pecans. Bake at 350°, 40 minutes. Loosen cake from rim of pan; cool before removing rim of pan. Chill. Garnish with whipped cream, additional chopped nuts and maraschino cherries, if desired.

10 to 12 servings

BROWNIE SWIRL CHEESECAKE

　　　1 8-ounce package brownie mix
　　　　　　*　　*　　*
　　　2 8-ounce packages PHILADELPHIA BRAND
　　　　　Cream Cheese, softened
　½ cup sugar
　　　1 teaspoon vanilla
　　　2 eggs
　　　1 cup milk chocolate pieces, melted

Grease bottom of 9-inch springform pan. Prepare basic brownie mix as directed on package; pour batter evenly into springform pan. Bake at 350°, 15 minutes.

Combine cream cheese, sugar and vanilla, mixing at medium speed on electric mixer until well blended. Add eggs, one at a time, mixing well after each addition. Pour over brownie layer. Spoon chocolate over cream cheese mixture; cut through batter with knife several times for marble effect. Bake at 350°, 35 minutes. Loosen cake from rim of pan; cool before removing rim of pan. Chill. Garnish with whipped cream, if desired.

10 to 12 servings

COCONUT CHOCO CHEESECAKE

　　　1 cup graham cracker crumbs
　　　3 tablespoons sugar
　　　3 tablespoons PARKAY Margarine, melted
　　　　　　*　　*　　*
　　　2 1-ounce squares unsweetened chocolate
　　　2 tablespoons PARKAY Margarine
　　　2 8-ounce packages PHILADELPHIA BRAND
　　　　　Cream Cheese, softened
1¼ cups sugar
　¼ teaspoon salt
　　5 eggs
1⅓ cups (3.5 ounce can) flaked coconut
　　　　　　*　　*　　*
　　　1 cup sour cream
　　　2 tablespoons sugar
　　　2 tablespoons brandy

(continued)

194

Combine crumbs, sugar and margarine. Press onto bottom of 9-inch springform pan. Bake at 350°, 10 minutes.

Melt chocolate and margarine over low heat, stirring until smooth. Cool. Combine cream cheese, sugar and salt, mixing at medium speed on electric mixer until well blended. Add eggs, one at a time, mixing well after each addition. Blend in chocolate mixture and coconut; pour over crust. Bake at 350°, 55 to 60 minutes or until set.

Combine sour cream, sugar and brandy; spread over cheesecake. Bake at 300°, 5 minutes. Loosen cake from rim of pan; cool before removing rim of pan. Chill.

10 to 12 servings

CHOCOLATE ORANGE SUPREME CHEESECAKE

1 cup chocolate wafer crumbs

$1/4$ teaspoon cinnamon

3 tablespoons PARKAY Margarine, melted

*   *   *

4 8-ounce packages PHILADELPHIA BRAND
    Cream Cheese, softened

$3/4$ cup sugar

4 eggs

$1/2$ cup sour cream

1 teaspoon vanilla

$1/2$ cup semi-sweet chocolate pieces, melted

2 tablespoons orange flavored liqueur

$1/2$ teaspoon grated orange peel

Combine crumbs, cinnamon and margarine; press onto bottom of 9-inch springform pan. Bake at 325°, 10 minutes.

Combine cream cheese and sugar, mixing at medium speed on electric mixer until well blended. Add eggs, one at a time, mixing well after each addition. Blend in sour cream and vanilla. Blend chocolate into 3 cups batter; blend liqueur and peel into remaining batter. Pour chocolate batter over crust. Bake at 350°, 30 minutes. Reduce oven temperature to 325°. Spoon remaining batter over chocolate batter; continue baking 30 minutes. Loosen cake from rim of pan; cool before removing rim of pan. Chill.

10 to 12 servings

INDEX